Black Officer, White Army

A MEMOIR OF

FORGIVENESS AND TOLERANCE

CYNTHIA RENÉ DOSS

Published by Muses and Graces Publishing Buena Park, California

Print ISBN: 979-8-35094-303-0
eBook ISBN: 979-8-35094-304-7

www.cynthiadoss.com

COMMENTS ABOUT THE AUTHOR

Cynthia Doss' story of her father is a reminder of the individuals among us who possess quiet modesty which unfortunately allows their accomplishments to be overlooked and under celebrated. Her father kept the details of his life achievements to himself only to be uncovered by his inquisitive daughter. It is a journey not to be missed. *~Jeff Duclos, Senior Editor, C Force*

A sobering and important take on a turbulent time in American history as seen through the eyes of a young Black woman who is determined to be a force of cultural change. *~Lisa Udelson, Writer/Director, Filmmaker*

So much of memoir these days is dedicated to sharing the darker sides of family life; i.e. questionable parenting, abuse. This memoir is a breath of fresh air. It does not shy away from the truth, but highlights the warmth, love and gratitude Cynthia Doss has for her father and family. *~Trish Cantillon, Essayist*

The Doss Family 1963
Seated L to R: Devereaux, Curtis Sr., Cynthia, Abiatha
Standing: Cyril, Curtis Jr.

October 16, 1968

A Timeline of 1968:

The Year That Shattered America

At the Olympic games in Mexico City, Americans Tommie Smith and John Carlos received gold and bronze medals in the 200-meter dash, then raised fists during the national anthem to protest violence toward and poverty among African-Americans. The next day, the Olympic Committee stripped their medals and sent them home.

~EXCERPT FROM SMITHSONIANMAG.COM

CHAPTER 1

"Girl, what is that?" my father asked, pointing to my blue jeans as I returned to my seat on the couch after changing the television channel. Whenever I got bored in class, which unfortunately was often, I drew designs on my jeans in ink. Mostly flowers and decorative doodles, but I had also written, "Black Power!"

It was 1968, and I was eleven years old. My father and I were in the basement den of our Junction City, Kansas, home. My father had finished the basement walls with plywood paneling and the always-cold cement floor with linoleum. On the far wall, he built shelves that were now filled with books and surrounded an opening where the television sat. Daddy was seated in his recliner reading his *U.S. News & World Report* magazine. He was dressed in his at-home uniform, a V-neck white T-shirt, khaki slacks, and brown corduroy house slippers.

"What's that on your leg?" he repeated with a stern look on his face.

At the time, I already knew the contributions of Black people in this country went well beyond the brief references to Crispus Attucks and George Washington Carver in my school textbooks. I already knew my ancestors and millions of other Black people were tightly woven into the fabric of what makes America, America.

With the exuberance of a well-read, socially conscious preteen who spent far too much time in the library, I began telling my father the reasons why I hated white people.

"They sold our ancestors as slaves like cattle. They raped our women and brutalized our men. They forced us to work and live under inhumane conditions. To this day, they don't consider us to be equals as American citizens. They've denied us opportunities for education, housing, employment, and any kind of advancement."

"That may be true of some white people," Daddy said. "But you can't harden your heart against any group of people." My eyes widened. This was coming from a man who was raised under Jim Crow laws in rural Arkansas during the Depression. A man who told me that if he ever looked a white person directly in the eye or talked back, he could have been beaten or lynched because that was the law.

"But you taught me to be proud of being Black."

"Yes, I did," he said. "As a Black person, you are not inferior to any race." He pointed his finger at me. "But that does not mean you're superior to anyone either. I've taught you to always stand up for yourself, but not by putting other people down." I sat down in the chair where my mother usually sat across from him as he continued. "Your mama and I made a point of traveling around Europe when I was stationed in Germany so you children would be exposed to different people and situations. You will come across people in life who have values and opinions that aren't the same as yours. If you make judgements about them, it should be based on their individual actions, not what race, ethnicity, or background they come from. I don't want to hear you talk any more about who you hate. Hate only makes you a bitter, angry person. It will eat away at you from the inside and rob you of the ability to enjoy life. Do you understand that?"

"Yes, sir," I replied quietly.

I always wondered how this gentle soul of a man managed to serve twenty-one years as a soldier in the United States Army. He rarely spoke of his service to us kids. I once asked him, "Daddy, what do you do at work?"

He looked up at me over his black-framed government-issued glasses.

"I drink coffee and tell men what to do," he replied, then flashed his 75-watt smile at me. The brightness of his smile contrasted against his dark complexion. At that point, my father, Curtis Doss Sr., was due to retire the following year after having achieved the rank of Chief Warrant Officer 3. Chief warrant officers are advanced level experts responsible for providing leadership of subordinate personnel, as well as technical and tactical advice to command staff. They are promoted up through the ranks of the United States Army after having demonstrated technical skill and leadership ability.

His response did not satisfy me.

It was more my father's nature to gain people's trust and cooperation than to boss them around. I also sensed he minimized his accomplishments, a feeling that was confirmed soon after when my mother told me that Daddy was responsible for the day-to-day operations of the motor pool at Fort Riley, home of the 1st Infantry Division. The motor pool performed maintenance on everything from jeeps to tanks to massive guns capable of blasting aircraft out of the sky. At all times, equipment had to be ready for deployment across the United States and internationally.

Because I never received more than quips from my father, like the one about drinking coffee, my curiosity about his work grew more intense as the years went by. In our family, it was considered impertinent for a child to ask too many questions. We weren't supposed to concern ourselves with what my parents called "grown folks' business." It was only after my father died in 2015 that I felt free to submit a formal request for his military service record.

I was overwhelmed when the National Archives delivered more than 500 documents to my mailbox.

With my childhood memories, some historical data, and Daddy's service record, I set out to piece together the story of his military service and understand how his experiences informed the way he raised me. The more I learned about the challenges my father faced transitioning from the segregated United States Army to the newly integrated United States Army, and through the turbulent 1960s, the more my respect for his strength of character grew. In a letter Daddy wrote to me and my siblings in 1998, he said, "If I were asked today 'would you serve again, if needed,' my answer would be 'where and when?'" No matter what they threw at him, he handled it with unparalleled grace and dignity.

My father always gave people the benefit of the doubt and trusted everyone. If someone slighted him, he would let it go, whereas I'd be in the process of plotting revenge. I'd ask, "Daddy, aren't you mad?" But he would shake it off.

"Nah, it's like water on a duck's back," he'd reply. The fact that he could be so forgiving absolutely infuriated me because I suspected I could never be as good a Christian, as good a human being, as he was.

Power isn't control at all – power is strength,
and giving that strength to others.
A leader isn't someone who forces others to make him
stronger; a leader is someone willing to give his strength
to others that they may be able to stand on their own.

~BETH REVIS

CHAPTER 2

The Gift

Though two years had now passed since my father died in 2015, I still felt pain at the loss of him every day. After having worked nearly forty years in the public sector, I was due to retire in a couple of years as a management analyst. I devoted much of my free time to conducting research. With my father's military record in hand, I began combing internet databases and library records, trying to locate information on the 76th Anti-Aircraft Artillery Battalion, the outfit he fought with in Korea. Specifically, I wanted to know more about the five campaigns for which he received decorations. But after weeks of searching, I had nothing to show for my efforts. Frustrated, I called my oldest brother Cyril. He served twenty-two years in the United States Navy, and I thought he could give me some insight.

"Cynthia, you have to realize when Daddy joined the service in 1947, the military was still segregated," he said. "White people didn't think it was necessary to document the contributions of what they called 'the colored units' because they believed they didn't matter." As he continued, I covered my eyes and shook my head, not wanting to believe people could be so callous. "There are Black soldiers, particularly the ones who served in Korea, who are only just now receiving posthumous recognition for bravery. For the ones who survived the war, when the segregated units were dissolved, they were reassigned, and if they had achieved any rank in the segregated units, they usually had to start from the bottom in their new units."

It was like a switch flipped inside my head, and a light turned on.

"So I'm beating my head against the wall for nothing," I said.

"Not necessarily. I'm just trying to warn you not to expect too much information to be available in the records."

I hung up the phone, and as I sat there thinking, I recalled a conversation many years prior. After I finished college, I was a volunteer advocate for the Rape Crisis Intervention Team (RCT) at Geary Community Hospital in Junction City in the early 1980s. Our training exposed us to what a rape victim could experience dealing with healthcare professionals, law enforcement, and the courts. I wasn't surprised when I received a call from a secretary arranging a meeting for me with the administrator of Geary Community Hospital, Jerry Aurbaugh. I anticipated it was probably a rah-rah-welcome-to-the-crisis-team talk.

I entered Mr. Aurbaugh's office to find him seated behind a hefty oak desk. When he stood up, I had to muffle a small gasp. He was at least six feet, three inches tall, maybe even six foot four, and powerfully built—not what I expected for an administrator. He had light brown hair that was slightly gray at the temples. I guessed from his name that he might have been of German descent.

He rounded the desk, and I swear it only took him two steps before he was in front of me.

"Hi, I'm Cynthia," I said, extending my hand. When he clasped both his hands around mine, my hand disappeared. His handshake was firm, but not crippling the way some men squeeze when they want to exert their authority.

"I'm Jerry Aurbaugh. Please have a seat." I sat down on a comfortable office chair while he returned to his desk.

"I wanted to take a few minutes to welcome you to the Rape Crisis Intervention Team or RCT, as we like to call it. RCT provides a vital service to victims. The process of dealing with doctors, law enforcement, and prosecutors can be overwhelming for a victim. We need advocates like you who can walk the victim through what they can expect and provide support throughout the process."

"Well, I'm happy to help," I said.

He finished his rah-rah-welcome-to-the-crisis-team speech. Then the conversation shifted in an unexpected direction.

"You know, I've been working with your dad for a number of years." I thought, *No, actually, I didn't know that.* He continued, "Mr. Doss has been a valuable asset to the hospital's board of directors."

W*hat?* Daddy never told me he was on the hospital board of directors. He said he was volunteering at the hospital. I knew he was active in Disabled American Veterans (DAV) and visited veterans in the hospital frequently. He never said a single word about being on the board of directors, but it was typical of him not to tell me the full extent of his involvement. I caught myself before my forehead formed a frown and gave away my bewilderment. Instead, I sat there dumbfounded, smiling and nodding, pretending to know what the hell this man was talking about.

"I'm retired United States Army like your dad. And although we never served together, I know the caliber of officer your dad must have been. He is from a generation of warrant officers who brought smoke. Regardless of the circumstances, they got the job done." I shifted in my chair and found myself leaning forward as he continued. "And it couldn't have been easy for him. Especially during integration of the service in the 1960s. To put it mildly, there are white men who don't like the idea of taking orders from a Black man. But I'm sure your father's knowledge base and positive demeanor inspired his men with confidence in his leadership ability."

Wow!

At that point in time, Daddy had been retired from the United States Army twelve years and was working as an auto mechanics teacher at Junction City High School. Though he didn't tell us kids much about his military experiences, occasionally I overheard him discussing specifics with other veterans—veterans like Mr. Aurbaugh, I imagined.

"Yes, my father is a pretty special person."

"Well, I hope you find your work on the RCT rewarding, and let me know if I can help in any way."

"Thank you. It was really nice meeting you, Mr. Aurbaugh," I said and excused myself.

Before going home, I stopped off at my parents' house. I found Daddy seated at the patio table in the backyard. He was sorting a cardboard box full of nuts and bolts by size and placing them in baby food jars.

"Hey, fella. How ya doin'?" My father always used "fella" and "buddy" in a non-gender-specific way. It was a term of endearment. I didn't even greet him.

"How come you didn't tell me you were on the board at Geary Community?"

He cracked a half-smile. "I told you I was volunteering . . ." he started.

"I thought that was DAV stuff. You never said you were on the board of directors. I just spent a half hour listening to the administrator tell me what a great guy you are and pretending like I knew what the heck he was talking about."

He raised his eyebrows and shrugged his shoulders. "It's not a big deal. Besides, your mama doesn't like me to talk about it."

His last statement deflated some of my frustration with him. His reluctance to talk about it was more than just his usual humility. Mommy considered any talk of achievements to be vanity and, therefore, a sin—the exception being when she was the one in the limelight. I couldn't be upset with him anymore.

"Now grab a crescent wrench and help me size these," he said.

Two weeks later, I was talking to Jen, the RCT program director, in her office.

"I had my meeting with your boss, Jerry Aurbaugh, a few weeks ago. He's a very pleasant man."

"What meeting?"

"You know, the meeting that's part of the training."

Her eyes widened, and she asked hesitantly, "What did the two of you talk about?"

I shared the encouraging words he gave me about the program and what he said about Daddy.

"Cynthia, meeting with the hospital administrator is not part of the training. I think he just wanted an opportunity to tell you how he felt about your dad."

Mr. Aurbaugh gave me a tremendous gift that day —the ability to see my father from the perspective of another career United States Army soldier. When I walked out of Mr. Aurbaugh's office, I knew I would no longer be satisfied with Daddy's vague answers about his service. In the years that followed, my desire to learn more about my father's career never left me. I wanted—no, I *needed* to know details.

Truth is power and it prevails.

~SOJOURNER TRUTH

CHAPTER 3

Mandate

In the beginning of 2018, I wrote several chapters to begin my father's story. I submitted the chapters to a writers' workshop. Eight other writers in the class sat around a conference room table and each took turns commenting on my work. Most felt I had adequately captured the close relationship I had with my father and the tremendous loss I suffered when he died. There were suggestions on places where I could expand the story, sections to be clarified, military terms that needed to be explained—the usual kind of comments offered in a writers' workshop.

One person's comments stood out. His name was Harry. Harry was a university statistics professor and delivered his comments slumped in his chair with his hands arched in a pyramid almost covering his face. He said my scenes were detailed and family relationships well described. He also suggested I drop the military aspect of the story. If I focused on my family relationships, he believed it would be a more compelling memoir because what I had learned in my research was my father was just a grunt in the United States Army, and his military job was inconsequential and boring.

I could not believe my ears. I kept my head down and didn't react. I continued to write notes as I had been all along as people gave their comments. But in my notebook, I wrote, *You smug, condescending little shit!* Then it was my turn to speak.

"Thank you all for your comments. But to be clear, my father retired as a Chief Warrant Officer 3 (CW3). My father's United States Army career is a huge part of this story."

Several people around the table nodded their heads.

Since workshop protocol dictates you should not attack anyone personally, I deliberately looked in the opposite direction from Harry as I continued. "But I find it interesting that an assumption was made that because he was a Black man, he had to be a private, or actually I believe the term used was 'grunt.' And it was further indicated that his work was inconsequential." When my father served, the Secretary of the Army awarded him the rank of CW3, and it was the highest rank my father could achieve in his field. Daddy's area of expertise was personnel training, equipment maintenance, and equipment deployment logistics. His overall mission was to consistently maintain the combat-readiness of motorized vehicles to include trucks, tanks, as well as antiaircraft guns and missile launchers.

As the workshop continued, and we commented on another writer's work, I caught a glimpse of Harry out of the corner of my eye. He sat upright in his seat now, and his face was flushed.

Many white people in this country probably would have made the same assumption as Harry. My encounter with him made me realize it is even more important that I tell my father's story; it is my mandate.

January 20, 1961

I do not shrink from this responsibility. I welcome it. I do not believe that any of us would exchange places with any other people or any other generation. The energy, the faith, the devotion which we bring to this endeavor will light our country and all who serve it. And the glow from that fire can truly light the world.

And so, my fellow Americans: ask not what your country can do for you, ask what you can do for your country.

~EXCERPT FROM PRESIDENT JOHN F. KENNEDY'S
INAUGURAL ADDRESS, ARCHIVES.GOV

CHAPTER 4

Ansbach, Germany

It was 1961, and my family and I were stationed at the United States Army Garrison in Ansbach, Germany. Our family consisted of my parents, Curtis Senior and Abiatha, brother Cyril (age nine), brother Curtis Junior (age six), me (age four), and my baby sister Devereaux (age two). Between the few things my young mind retained and pictures my parents took at the time, I have been able to stitch together select memories.

Our United States Army housing was a three-bedroom apartment: one bedroom for the boys, one bedroom for the girls, my parents' room, a living room, small dining area, and kitchen. My world at the time was limited to mealtimes, playground time, and naptime. By far the brightest moment of my day was when my father walked through the door after work. His arrival times varied depending on his duty assignment, but most days he was home in time for dinner.

His five-foot-ten frame burst through the front door wearing his United States Army olive drab uniform fatigues. Though he had a slender build, the lofty field jacket made him look like a big bear. The jacket was covered in patches and insignias and his Sargent First Class or E-6 stripes. I wouldn't learn the significance of those symbols until later in life as an adult. His fatigue pants were carefully tucked into calf-high, highly polished black combat boots that laced up the front. He dropped his leather satchel and gear at the front door with a thud. Black government-issued glasses framed his wide brown eyes. His complexion was the color of rich chocolate. A neatly trimmed black mustache was perched above his upper lip. His lips parted into a smile so wide I could count his molars when he saw me.

"Daddy!" I shouted and ran toward him with my arms outstretched.

"Hi, buddy," he said. I felt his bicep muscle flex as he scooped me up with his right arm. I wrapped my arms tightly around his neck. I kissed him on the cheek, then rubbed my nose. The stubble from his five o'clock shadow tickled. By now, Devereaux had toddled over and was pulling on his pant leg. He reached down and scooped her up with his left arm.

My mother came out of the kitchen drying her hands on her apron. She was an expert seamstress and made a collection of printed cotton aprons to coordinate with solid color A-line dresses and sheaths. She stood a few inches shorter than Daddy with a lighter complexion, but not fair-skinned. Her jet-black hair flipped up at the ends Jackie Kennedy–style as it graced her shoulders. Her almond-shaped eyes brightened at the sight of Daddy.

"Hi Bidey, give me some sugar," he said. Bidey was the nickname my mother's family gave her. Daddy seldom called her Abiatha. She leaned in and kissed him.

"Hi, yourself," she responded and to us said, "You two need to let your daddy get settled in. He hasn't even taken his hat off yet."

Daddy put us down on the floor, and I waited impatiently as he went to their bedroom to get comfortable. When he returned several minutes later, he was wearing a white T-shirt and his fatigue pants but had traded his combat boots for a pair of corduroy house slippers. His aluminum dog tags still hung around his neck as he sunk into his side chair in the living room with a sigh.

The living room furnishings included a sofa, coffee table, and two overstuffed side chairs adorned with doilies. Next to each side chair was an end table with a lamp. Also, a German console radio my parents had purchased stood in a corner. It was taller than me and took up most of the corner. A turntable that played 33-, 45-, and 78-speed vinyl records was recessed in the top of the console. Radio programming options available at the time were German polka music, Armed Forces Network news, and German polka music. A lively polka tune played softly in the background as Daddy motioned for Devereaux and I to join him in his chair. He placed one of us on each knee while Cyril and Curtis ran their toy cars and dump trucks across the floor, simulating crashes and making motor noises with their lips.

A wonderful aroma wafted from the kitchen as Mommy put the final touches on dinner. Daddy was having a different dinner of sorts. He acted like he had a salt shaker in his hand and shook pretend salt on my ear. He then wrapped his lips around his teeth and began chewing my ear.

"Mmm, good stuff," he said. The combination of feeling his warm breath in my ear and the tickle of his mustache on my cheek made me giggle with delight. When he finished with my ear, he turned to Devereaux and continued his feast.

While he tickled Devereaux, I took my finger and traced the features of his face: the creases that appeared on either side of his mouth when he smiled, the wiry hair of his bushy eyebrows, the stubble on his cheeks and jawline, and finally his wide, somewhat bulbous, nose. Years later, as an adolescent, I would pinch my nose every single night and pray, *Dear Lord, I love everything about my father, but please don't give me his nose.* But at four years old, sitting on his knee, looking up at Daddy's face, every feature was perfect.

I lifted the two silver-colored metal dog tags that always hung on a ball chain around Daddy's neck. I traced the imprint of letters on the tags with my finger. I had no way of knowing their significance at the time. No way of knowing their purpose was to identify his body if he were to become a casualty in combat. In my blissful ignorance, I relaxed my head on his shoulder and inhaled the scent of him. He smelled of calm, and of safety, and of Old Spice aftershave. Short of one failed experiment with Brut for Men in the 1970s, my father only wore Old Spice. The fragrance hypnotized me until Mommy's voice broke the spell.

"Okay, playtime's up. Y'all come get your dinner." Somehow, I wasn't disappointed that this special time with Daddy was ending. Over time, he would prove to me that he would always be there for me—to flash a quick smile to make me laugh, poke me in the side to tickle me, or encourage me when school got the better of me. So today I am amazed this gentle soul who taught me to ride my first bicycle and helped me with homework on school nights, could have been a soldier in the United States Army for twenty-one years. And that he fought in the Korean War. Daddy wasn't intentionally secretive about his service, just humble.

February 24, 1964

Cassius Clay (Muhammad Ali) defeats Sonny Liston
and becomes World Heavy Weight Boxing Champion.

CHAPTER 5

Rescue Mission

After a brief return to the United States, my father was assigned to Germany again in 1964. This time he was with the 89th Transportation Company, 53rd Transportation Battalion at Kaiserslautern. We traveled on the ocean liner USS Buckner from New York City to Bremen, Germany. The trip took about six or seven days. I have only two memories from our transatlantic voyage. When they called all passengers out on deck for an emergency drill soon after the ship was underway, I was terrified. I had a death fear of high places and large bodies of water since I could not swim. We were wearing overcoats under our life jackets because it was very windy on deck. My brothers wore German fedoras they had gotten when Daddy was previously assigned to Germany. I stood on one side of Mommy, and Devereaux stood on the other. That was always the division of labor: Mommy looked out for us girls, Daddy the boys. As I clung to Mommy's waist, a crew member walked by. He admonished my mother for not providing hats for us girls. I was only seven years old but old enough to know he had been disrespectful to my mother, and I glared at him in anger.

The second memory is Devereaux, then five years old, suffered a sickle cell anemia (SCA) crisis on board. Sickle cell anemia is a disease that changes normal red blood cells into the shape of a sickle. These abnormal cells carry less oxygen and block the passage of blood through the veins and arteries, further depriving the body of life-sustaining oxygen. At any given time, the amount of sickled blood cells in a body can be as much as 50 percent. When the percentage increases, the patient goes into a crisis. The patient experiences extreme pain and, in severe cases, internal organ failure.

As a child, when my friends would ask me what sickle cell felt like for my sister, I'd tell them, "Wrap a rubber band around your finger." After a few minutes, the tips of their fingers would turn white, and they would frown from the pain. "That's what it's like when a part of your body doesn't get the blood it needs."

There was no treatment for SCA at the time. My parents applied a hot water bottle to whatever part of her body was in pain and kept her hydrated. She was confined to our cabin for the duration of the trip, so my parents tried to find ways to entertain her. The ship had a library, and Daddy checked out several books. She was particularly fond of the story of a mouse called *Cheerful*. It had the cutest picture of a mouse on the cover, and my parents read it to her over and over again. When Daddy returned the books to the library at the end of the trip, he mentioned how much Devereaux enjoyed and how much it had helped her during her illness. The librarian told him to let her keep the book. Devereaux still has that book today.

When the ship docked in Germany, we traveled by car to a temporary home. Since there were no quarters available at the time for us on the base, we lived "on the economy." The term "on the economy" was used to refer to a local German neighborhood. We stayed there several weeks until our new home on the United States Army base at Kaiserslautern was ready.

Though my parents spoke fluent German, a result of Daddy being stationed in Germany for two previous assignments, I was only a toddler during his last tour of duty and didn't exactly pick up any of the language.

At the time, I was keenly aware of what the changes meant. I had been uprooted in the middle of the school year and planted in this completely unfamiliar environment. There would be no more catching tadpoles in the ravine at the end of our street in Junction City, Kansas. I would no longer be able to ride my bike with my friends to the Kwik Sak on the corner of Westwood Boulevard and 14th Street to buy a can of 7Up and bag of Lay's potato chips for thirty-five cents. I was no longer able to run around the open field at Filby Park catching butterflies that Mommy would only let me keep in the house if they were sealed in a jar. To Mommy, a butterfly was just a moth in a cute disguise.

I loved the makeup of our Junction City, Kansas, community. We had our own miniature United Nations because of the proximity to Fort Riley—an oasis in a desert. The remainder of the state of Kansas was predominantly white. At that age, I had little awareness of color barriers. I had friends of Japanese, Korean, Italian, Filipino, and German descent. It was cool to visit their homes, where a variety of languages were spoken and I learned their traditions. I had a healthy appetite and loved exploring the foods of different countries. But my friends were all gone now. I was transplanted in a place where everything was foreign to me.

On the first day at my new school in Kaiserslautern, Daddy took me to my second grade class. It was at an American elementary school on the base. Why Daddy took me, I don't know. Usually my mother did things like that. Daddy was dressed in his United States Army olive green fatigues, a loose-fitting field jacket, green pants tucked in calf-high, and spit-shined black combat boots. I don't remember my dress specifically, but I'm sure it was pretty. The bows on my braided pigtails matched my dress. A row of bangs was curled against my forehead. Laced, trimmed socks peeked out above black patent leather Mary Jane shoes. I'm certain that's what I wore because that's the way Mommy always dressed me. Daddy walked me into the classroom. He talked with the teacher briefly, said goodbye to me, and left.

The teacher introduced me to the class and led me to my desk. I tried to pay attention to what the teacher was saying but could not focus. I was shy, and all I could think about was how hard it would be to make friends in this new school. I missed our five-bedroom ranch house with a huge yard and fruit trees on a corner lot at Westwood Boulevard and Bel Air Drive. I missed my friends and my old school, especially the library. It was in the cozy confines of the Westwood Elementary School library that my lifelong love of books and reading was born.

Back in the Kaiserslautern classroom, I looked up. I could have sworn the walls of the room were moving closer and closer to me, and I began to cry. Even in my young mind I knew this wasn't like me. *Cynthia, you are not a crybaby. Stop it!* I told myself. But I could not stop. The teacher came over and tried to console me, but she eventually had to go back to teaching the class. I sat there sobbing for over an hour. My throat was now sore. I had run out of tears and was quietly whimpering when I heard a familiar voice.

"Hey, buddy. What's wrong?" I looked up, and Daddy stood beside me. I guess the teacher had given up and called him to come get me. His five-foot-ten-inch frame loomed over me like a giant. I threw my arms around him and held him tightly. He pried me away, wrapped both of his massive hands around my little one, and led me out to the car.

"I know this is a big adjustment for you, but if you give this new school a chance, you might like it," he said. "Reading was one of your favorite subjects, right?" I nodded. "Well, this school is going to teach you to read in German, as well as English. Doesn't that sound like fun?" The most I could manage was to shrug my shoulders.

On the way home, he continued to console me. I understood enough about his work to know it wasn't the kind of job you just walk away from saying, "Hey fellas, I'm gonna take off an hour or so to pick up my kid at school." I knew I had inconvenienced him, but he never once complained. If it had been my mother, I would have gotten an earful for hours. She would have criticized me for acting like a baby and interrupting her day to have to come get me. Then she would have retold the story of my first day at Kaiserslautern Elementary for the next thirty years, with increasing drama each time.

Daddy walked me to the door of the home where we were staying, and after a few words with my mother, he left. Mommy's slender figure stood in the doorway with her hands on her hips. At only thirty-six years old at the time, silver-gray hairs were already beginning to appear at her temples.

Mommy glared down at me and said, "I truly do not understand you. Why can't you act your age? Go to your room!" I always had the impression Mommy relished the time we were in school and not underfoot. I spent the rest of the day tucked away in my room playing with my Norfin trolls and coloring while Mommy went about her daily chores. It was okay. Sometimes it was better when she ignored me. The less she talked to me, the less she could criticize me.

While in my room, I resolved to never cry like that publicly ever again—a promise I kept until each of my parents died many decades later. School was something I loved. I would not allow fear to stand in the way of my enjoyment of something I loved. I had seen the movie *The Wizard of Oz* several times, but I clearly understood there would be no clicking my heels to return to Kansas. This was my new reality.

If you talk to a man in a language he understands,
that goes to his head.
If you talk to him in his language,
that goes to his heart.

~AUTHOR UNKNOWN

CHAPTER 6

Die, Der, Das

The fact that my parents were fluent in German offered many advantages. And my father was right: I did enjoy learning the German language in school. Over the years, though, I have lost most of what I learned as a child, and the process of relearning has been a struggle. For example, in English we can use the word "the" to introduce any noun. In German, "the" can be either *die*, *der*, or *das*, depending on the noun. It is a lot to remember. Challenges like that make me even more proud of my parents' talents.

I loved watching them interact with the locals when we traveled to places like Berchtesgaden, Frankfurt, Munich, and Heidelberg, where the night sky would light up with fireworks behind Heidelberg Castle. What intrigued me more than touring ornate castles were our trips into der Schwartzwald, the Black Forest. I'd think *Oooooo, the Black Forest*. It sounded both scary and exciting at the same time. The Black Forest is a 4,000-square-mile mountain range characterized by rivers, valleys, and rolling hills in Southwest Germany. Our adventures took us into the northern most part of the Black Forest as far as the town of Baden-Baden.

The dense green trees of the forest created a canopy, and the sun could be seen only through sporadic openings. When we drove into the forest, it took a few minutes for my eyes to adjust to the darkness. I was a little intimidated by the height of the trees and the closed-in feeling but still intrigued because I never knew what would be around the next corner. The forest was spotted with thatched-roof cottages with bay windows that had a fairy-tale vibe. It wasn't until later, as an adult, I learned my assessment was accurate. The Black Forest was where Grimms' Fairy Tale characters Hansel and Gretel met the wicked witch.

My second fascination was with the abundance of souvenir shops in the Black Forest. At seven or eight years old, I quickly tired of touring castles. Yet, I never tired of visiting souvenir shops . . . ever.

On one particular trip, my parents wanted to buy a clock for our home, so into the Black Forest we went. We drove down the main road that connected most of the shops. The headlights of our salmon-and-white-colored 1962 Rambler station wagon spilled onto the trunks of huge spruce trees on either side of us as we wound through the dense forest. Though each cottage shop had a thatched roof and some type of green vines or flower trellis on the front, no two buildings were shaped alike. I was excited to see what new structure the car's headlights would illuminate.

The Black Forest featured some of the best clockmakers in the country, particularly cuckoo clocks. After being in several stores when the hour hand struck, my parents were determined the cuckoo feature was not right for our family. Having a bird jump out of the clock and declare, "Cuckoo, cuckoo, cuckoo, cuckoo, cuckoo, cuckoo, cuckoo, cuckoo, cuckoo, cuckoo, cuckoo" at noon and midnight was clearly too disruptive. Eventually we happened upon a store that had the usual thatched roof with lattice on the facade, but unlike the other shops, not every inch of wall space inside was covered with cuckoo clocks.

The clerk was a short man with round glasses and round cheeks. He wore traditional German lederhosen: suspenders and a small bib attached to leather pants. He must have known we were not typical German customers as he greeted us in English.

"Good morning, may I help you find something?"

"*Guten morgen,*" Daddy said, "*Wir möchten eine Uhr für unser Zuhause kaufen.*" ("Good morning, we would like to buy a clock for our home.")

The man's face immediately brightened. He did not expect Daddy to speak his language.

"*Sehr gut, sehr gut. Eine Wanduhr oder Kaminuhr?*" ("Very good, very good. A wall clock or a mantle clock?")

Daddy glanced at Mommy for a second before responding, "*Eine Kaminuhr.*" ("A mantle clock.")

"*Gut, folge mir.*" ("Good, follow me.") The clerk walked around the counter to the side of the store and showed my parents a teak wood mantle clock. He moved the minute hand around until the hour hand landed on a number so they could hear the clock's Westminster chime. It was a melodious tune that touched my heartstrings. The wood case that housed the clock was a minimalist design, and the face of the clock had cardinal numbers instead of Roman numerals like the more ornate clocks. The design was clean and elegant. I loved it immediately. My parents looked at each other.

"*Wie viel kostet es?*" ("How much does it cost?") Mommy asked.

"*Einhundertzwanzig Deutsche Mark.*" ("One hundred and twenty Deutsche Marks.") The equivalent of thirty American dollars at the time.

Mommy tilted her head slightly, smiled at the clerk, and asked, "Würdest sie stattdessen hundert nehmen?" ("Would you take a hundred instead?") Between my parents, Mommy was definitely the negotiator. The clerk smiled.

"*Ya, ya, das ist gut,*" ("Yes, that is good") the clerk said, smiling back at Mommy.

"*Wir werden es nehmen,*" Daddy said. ("We'll take it.") The clerk began wrapping the clock, and Daddy paid him.

"*Danke schoen*," (Thank you very much) my parents said in unison, and we left.

Unfortunately, I do recall one incident when understanding the German language wasn't such an advantage. Our family was visiting a castle. Daddy had gone to the box office to buy tickets for our tour and left Mommy, Cyril, Curtis, Devereaux, and me in the car. While we waited, three nuns dressed in black-and-white habits walked by the car. They stopped for a moment and looked in the window. They smiled at us and began pointing and speaking in German. My brothers, sister, and I didn't understand what they were saying, but we smiled and waved back at them. They continued to point at us and began laughing before they walked away.

"Mommy, what were they saying?" Cyril asked. She abruptly turned her body toward the front windshield of the car.

"It was nothing," she said.

"Come on, Mommy, what were they saying?" Curtis asked, and Devereaux and I chimed in. Finally, she realized we were not going to let the issue drop.

"They were saying, 'Look at the cute little monkeys,'" she said. Her eyebrows were furrowed, and her lips were pulled tight.

"Monkeys? Why would they call us monkeys?" Curtis asked.

"Because you are Black," she said quietly. Mommy chose not to offer any further explanation of the nuns' actions, but she didn't have to. I was old enough to understand a racist remark. No one wanted to talk about it anymore.

As an adult, I asked Mommy if there were other incidents they chose not to tell us about.

"No," she said. "We experienced far more racism traveling in our own country than we ever did in Germany or other European countries."

My name can't be *that* tough to pronounce!

~KEANU REEVES

CHAPTER 7

Cynthia, Never Cindy

By the time I finished second grade at Kaiserslautern Elementary School, I had acclimated to my new German adventure. I still loved school. I earned good grades in all my classes except math, where I struggled hard for a satisfactory mark. Third grade was fun, and time seemed to pass quickly. Fourth grade was a different story.

The first day of school that year, Mrs. Petrovitch, a tall, stocky woman, introduced herself as our teacher. Most of the people who taught at United States Army bases overseas were either married to military service personnel or single seeking an adventure. After she began roll call, the teacher paused.

"It looks like we have two Cynthias in the class," she said. Can you both raise your hands?" A petite girl with curly blond hair and I complied with her request. She pointed to me and said, "To prevent confusion, we're going to call you Cindy." It was as if I physically heard a phonograph needle skip across the grooves of a record album.

My name is not Cindy, I thought. I was angry but too shy to tell her I didn't want this new name. As she continued roll call, I made a general assessment of her. I judged her to be middle-aged, but to my nine-year-old mind, all adults were either middle-aged or old. She wore a simple printed loose-fitting dress. I was used to the dresses my mother wore. Mommy dressed to flatter her figure. If Mrs. Petrovitch had a figure, it was hidden under her earth-tone frock. Because my mother color-coordinated my dresses, shoes, and accessories, I had already developed a keen eye for attractive colors. The muted earth tones Mrs. Petrovitch wore were not doing her any favors. They seemed to further drain color from the appearance of her pale complexion and shoulder-length dirty blond hair. Because I loved school so much, I didn't want to dislike Mrs. Petrovitch, but the seeds of discontent were sown on that first day.

One of the few good things that happened that year was I met and became friends with Lisa Blake. Lisa loved horses as much as I loved butterflies. On the weekends, she would tag along with me as I chased and captured butterflies that were drawn to the flower beds in front of our apartment building. Their bright, beautiful wings attracted me, but it was the freedom with which they flew through the sky that impressed me.

But school days were drudgery. Mrs. Petrovitch's disposition was pleasant most days, but her broad face had perpetual vertical lines between her eyebrows, as though she were always in serious contemplation. She rarely smiled. I don't remember the color of her eyes. I never wanted to get close enough to her to be able to tell.

I constantly struggled to complete my math homework. In the evenings, Daddy tried to help me. One night we worked through a series of problems. I had the sense, at times, that he was as baffled as I was, but he was willing to help, so I said nothing. I remember having to erase so often that the paper I was going to turn in wasn't as neat as most of my assignments. But I was happy I finished it.

The following day, I had a Girl Scout troop meeting after school, so I wore my uniform to class. I turned my homework assignments in to Mrs.

Petrovitch as I entered class. In first period, she allowed us to read silently while she graded homework.

When it came time for our math lesson, Mrs. Petrovitch returned our homework to us. She handed my paper to me. It had a huge red "F" on it. I had never received a failing grade in my life. I looked up at her in disbelief.

"Cindy, your mother helped you with your homework, didn't she?" she asked.

"No, ma'am," I said still stunned from the grade.

"She must have helped you. That's why I can't give you any credit for the assignment."

Mrs. Petrovitch's assertions were ridiculous in my mind. My mother never helped me with homework because she didn't have the patience. It was ironic because Mommy handled all the family finances and was a wiz at economizing to make my father's salary stretch to meet the needs of six people. I continued to deny I had any help from Mommy. Mrs. Petrovitch's body stiffened, and she quickly walked to the front of the class.

"Class, can I have your attention, please?" When the talking stopped and everyone settled down, she continued. "Class, I need to talk to you about something serious. Cindy has denied that her mother helped her with her homework when I have evidence that she did. For her to sit there in a Girl Scout uniform and lie to me is a disgrace. She does not deserve to wear the uniform."

I was furious. I had not lied. My mother had not helped me with homework. My father helped me, and that's a huge difference to a nine-year-old kid. Also, what would be wrong with a parent helping a child with homework? I thought that was what parents were supposed to do. I could not respond to her attack. I was too angry to speak. My forehead was so hot I felt like an egg would fry on it.

In our home, there were three words my siblings and I were not allowed to call each other. The words were "stupid," "dumb," and "liar." My parents judged the words to be incredibly hurtful. I sat there glaring at Mrs. Petrovitch.

The anger of that moment remained with me for over fifty years. In my professional life, if someone wanted to criticize the quality of my work, I had no problem. I would always consider the legitimacy of their comment. However, I never allowed anyone to question my integrity. Also, whenever I was introduced to someone new, they would often refer to me as Cindy. I corrected them immediately. "My name is Cynthia, not Cindy." If the person continued to call me Cindy, I made sure I locked my eyes on theirs and slowly said, "My name is Cynthia, never Cindy."

In my sixty-six years on this planet, I have never had a Black person call me Cindy. Only white people do that. I find that interesting.

Since I knew I had done nothing wrong, I continued to wear my Girl Scout uniform to school whenever necessary. When Mrs. Petrovitch realized she hadn't succeeded in shaming me, she tried to take advantage of other opportunities to try to embarrass me. She seemed to only call on me in class when I didn't know the answer. At first I thought it was my dumb luck that she caught me off guard. Then one day she asked a difficult math question. I thought, *Please don't call on me. Please, please.* I broke eye contact with her and looked out the window.

"Cindy, surely you must know the answer," she said in a syrupy sweet voice.

"No, ma'am. I don't," I said. That's when it hit me. When I looked away, she suspected I didn't know the answer.

To test my theory, whenever I didn't have the answer to a question, I smiled slightly and made sure my eyes locked on hers like a heat-seeking missile. The result was she didn't call on me. Conversely, when I was certain

I knew the correct answer, I immediately broke eye contact with her and looked at something else in the room.

"Cindy, can you tell us the capital of Argentina?" she once asked with a wide smile.

"The capital of Argentina is . . . ah . . ." I hesitated, pretending I was unsure. Her smile widened. "The capital of Argentina is Buenos Aires."

"That's right," she said slowly. The corners of her mouth dropped.

As time went on, the more correct answers I gave her, the less she would call on me. Even when I raised my hand in response to a question, she ignored me. I didn't tell my parents about my fourth grade experience. My father was generous enough to try to help me with my homework. I didn't want him to know the help he gave me caused a problem in class. Besides, Mrs. Petrovitch was the problem, not my father.

In the early years of the Viet Nam War, Blacks and working-class whites were being shipped to combat assignments in record numbers. Project 100,000 was initiated in 1966 aimed at drafting 100,000 additional military personnel per year. Blacks comprised 40 percent of Project 100,000 draftees, though only 11 percent of the American population at the time was Black.

~UNITED STATES DEPARTMENT OF DEFENSE

CHAPTER 8

Summertime, but the Livin' Ain't Easy

We had been back in the United States almost a year. The sun loomed high above, and if it weren't for the patio cover, Mommy and I would have been roasting as we sat on the cement back porch step of our Junction City, Kansas, home. Kansas summers were as brutal as the winters. I could see heat rising in waves from the concrete patio floor. My mother always said young ladies don't sweat; they perspire. But the short set I wore on my lanky ninety-pound frame was drenched in sweat, and the humidity made it hard for me to breathe. I was about twelve years old, and preparing fruit for canning was a ritual Mommy and I repeated every summer.

Three tin washtubs were displayed in front of us. One held peaches picked from our backyard trees; another held skins and pits; and the third, peeled fruit. I watched as Mommy twisted a peach and split it in half with her bare hands. She dug the pit out with her Swiss Army knife. The heavenly aroma rose and titillated my nostrils, making my mouth water. I raised the peach in my hand to my nose and inhaled deeply. The peach was perfectly ripe with the fragrant high notes of a fine French perfume. I closed my eyes and saw colorful bursts of pink, orange, and red, and I imagined the explosion of flavor that would greet my tongue. It took every ounce of resistance I had not to sink my teeth into the luscious fruit and let the juice dribble out of the sides of my mouth.

"Don't even think about it," Mommy said without looking in my direction.

"I could just test it for quality control," I said. Now Mommy glared at me like I had lost my natural mind.

"You've been watching too much television," she said, then muttered, "Quality control," under her breath. She peeled the fuzz from each peach half and deposited the juicy fruit in the appropriate washtub. She used the back of her hand to sweep a long tendril of her black hair away from her face. Beads of sweat dotted her chestnut brown forehead.

We had been sitting for over an hour, mostly in silence. It was too hot even for insects to chirp. My poor fat-free butt cheeks were beginning to burn, but I knew my complaint would not have been well received. Mommy was raised in the Depression. My easy life was no comparison to her hardships. Decades later, through genealogical research, I would learn that Mommy's father's grandmother—my great-great grandmother—made the arduous trek by covered wagon in 1891 from Raleigh, North Carolina, to Emerson, Arkansas, with her family. I can only imagine what they must have endured: heat, cold, wild animals, bandits, hunger, thirst. Mommy was the descendent of pioneer women.

At the time, all I knew was it was better to suck it up and suffer in silence than to appear to be a weakling. And over time, I figured out that if I shifted my weight from one butt cheek to the other, I could lessen the burn and prevent my legs from completely going to sleep. I picked up a peach that was badly bruised. The sticky flesh of the fruit oozed between my fingers and sent a chill up my spine.

"Yuck," I said and tossed the peach in the tub with the peels and pits.

"Whoa, what are you doing? There is some good fruit left on that one. Pick that up."

I obliged, and as Mommy directed me, I cut away the bruised spots. A worm emerged. He squirmed around violently, angry I had disturbed his mealtime. A wet belch started in the back of my throat. I gagged and wanted to throw up but knew Mommy would be furious. I swallowed and took a few breaths to calm myself. I continued to cut to get rid of the worm and let out a sigh of relief when it was in the discard tub.

"We can't afford to throw away good food," Mommy said.

After a long period of silence, I said, "There were more casualties on the news last night." When we were stationed in Kaiserslautern, Germany, and I was about nine years old, I remember adults saying the words Viet Nam. I didn't know it was a country, and I sure as hell didn't know there was a war going on there. It seems unfathomable today when volumes of information are available with just a few clicks on the computer, but my parents were able to prevent us from knowing the potential dangers of Daddy's work. However, when we returned to the United States in the fall of 1967, they could no longer keep us isolated.

When I learned about Viet Nam in social studies class, I was shocked. I began reading whatever I could in the newspaper. Also, every night Walter Cronkite updated me on not just the war, but the Civil Rights Movement, the Women's Movement, and the massacre at the Munich Summer Olympics.

"I don't like you watching the news so much," Mommy said. She rinsed her knife and slowly honed it on a sharpening stone.

"We're studying the war in school."

"Yes, but you know that kind of thing gives you nightmares." She was right. The images of wounded men being loaded into helicopters on stretchers stayed with me a long time, invaded my dreams, and caused me to wake up screaming at night.

Mommy frowned and stared at the cement patio floor as if she were playing out a scene in her mind. She started to say something, then as if she thought better of it, shook her head.

"I don't want to talk about this anymore," she said. I would be an adult before Mommy would tell me that at one point, my father received orders for Viet Nam. For now, she silently showed me for the zillionth time how to peel the outer peach fuzz, leaving the maximum amount of juicy fruit behind. Her face brightened.

"I bought the fabric for that peasant dress you wanted. It's a nice floral pattern. I think you'll like it."

"Nice," I said.

Preparing fruit during canning season cheated me out of summer fun each year. Not only was it messy and gross; I wasn't allowed to explore the neighborhood on my bike with my friends or catch butterflies at Filby Park. Today, however, I value the time spent learning from the most resilient woman I have ever known.

January 2, 1969

Stage play, *To Be Young, Gifted and Black*, adapted from Lorraine Hansberry's writings, premieres in New York City.

CHAPTER 9

Farmer Doss

Though our hometown of Junction City, Kansas, was not rural, we benefitted from the numerous farms of various sizes that surrounded us. Since my parents were both raised on farms, they took advantage of any opportunity to buy fresh eggs, butter, even a side of beef on one occasion. Mommy had a fascination with pullet eggs. Pullets are young hens, and the eggs they lay are smaller and have more colorful shells than the eggs we would buy at the Commissary on Post. The intensely colored yolks of the eggs are more orange than yellow and offer a fresher flavor. Besides those advantages, I think Mommy just liked saying the word "pullet."

So when Daddy came home from work one day with a crate with two hens in it, I wasn't totally surprised. I thought, *Great, now we'll have fresh eggs all the time*. He had tucked his tie into the front of his short-sleeve pale blue dress shirt to keep it out of his way as he unloaded the crate from the back of his red Ford F-Series truck. Daddy set the chickens loose in the backyard and after saying a quick hello to me, went into the house.

Our house sat on a quarter-acre corner lot enclosed by a chain link fence. I was fourteen years old at the time and was playing in the backyard with our two dogs Tom and Geri. Tom was a chihuahua mix with large, pointed ears that were out of proportion to his puny head. True to his chihuahua nature, he immediately started barking relentlessly when he saw the intruders in his space, and the chase was on. His sister Geri, on the other hand, a dachshund mix, barked a few times, then waddled up to the back porch step and sat next to me. She was a round, barrel-shaped dog that seldom got excited or moved any more than she had to, God bless her.

Geri and I sat for about ten to fifteen minutes in the shade of the patio watching as Tom chased the chickens. They evaded him at each turn but squawked to high heaven whenever he got close. Then it hit me: If Tom kept up this pace, the poor little chickens would run their legs off. I needed to distract him, which wasn't hard to do because he had the attention span of a gnat on crack. I tossed one of his balls in the yard, and he began fetching it back to me. Problem solved.

The chickens stopped squawking and walked the perimeter of the yard, investigating their new home. I loved watching how their necks bobbed with the red fleshy skin under their beak flapping back and forth as they walked. They were the epitome of cool. And since we had a Tom and Geri, I continued the cartoon theme and named them Heckle and Jeckle.

It was approaching five o'clock when Mommy poked her head out the back screen door.

"We need to get dinner started," she said. That was the royal "we" because by then, I alone cooked the family meals.

"Aren't they cute?" I asked pointing to the chickens in the corner of the yard. "I named them Heckle and Jeckle."

Mommy frowned. She was not impressed. "Come on inside and get started."

"Okay," I said, reluctantly leaving Geri to watch over my new friends.

After Mommy told me what to prepare for dinner, she disappeared downstairs. The menu that night consisted of macaroni and cheese, sliced Spam topped with peaches and broiled for a few minutes, and boiled broccoli and cauliflower. We boiled the shit out of every vegetable in those days. That's what Mommy taught me and the way she was taught and so on and so on.

While the broccoli and cauliflower were bubbling, I whipped two eggs with one cup of milk and a half a stick of melted butter and folded in three cups of shredded cheddar cheese. I then poured the mixture over cooked elbow macaroni in a square Pyrex dish and slid the dish in the 375-degree preheated oven. I set the timer for twenty minutes and was removing the Spam from the broiler when I heard one of the chickens squawk loudly for about fifteen seconds, then there was silence. My heart jumped. I was sure Tom had attacked and injured Heckle or Jeckle. I looked out the kitchen window but couldn't see either chicken in the yard. I rushed around the dining room table and looked out the screen door into the backyard.

One of the chickens lay motionless on newspaper spread out to cover the patio table. Her neck was stretched out, her head flopped over in a pool of blood. My father, the ultimate gentleman, courageous and kind, stood in the middle of the backyard with his back to me. He had changed into one of the coveralls he used to repair cars. He was holding the second chicken upside down by the legs. The bird flapped its wings ferociously, trying to break free of Daddy's grasp. She continued squawking as he raised her over his head and swung her in a circle. After a few rounds, he snapped his wrist in a way that reminded me of how my brothers used to wet the corner of a bath towel, twirl it lengthwise, and snap it at me to sting my skin. The bird's squawking ceased as bright red blood squirted across the lawn. Her neck was now extended and limp.

As Daddy turned to walk toward the patio table, I jumped back from the door. I didn't want him to know I had seen him kill Heckle and Jeckle. He would feel bad if he knew he had done something to upset me. I wanted to back away farther but couldn't get my body to move for a few moments. My heart was racing. I broke out in a cold sweat, and I heard a slight sizzling sound in my head. I felt like I was about to faint. I grabbed onto the china cabinet, dining room chairs, and other furniture for support to make it back to the kitchen. When I reached the sink, I splashed cold water on my face and laid a wet towel at the base of my neck. The sound in my head was lessening, and in a few minutes, the cold sweat had also passed. I finished preparing dinner in a trance.

Occasionally, I would look out the kitchen window at Daddy. He sat, calm as a coma, at the patio table plucking feathers off the chickens. *At least they won't make me do that*, I thought. It was bad enough I would have to cook them. Daddy finished by chopping the heads and feet off and wrapping the hens in Saran Wrap, then butcher paper. When he came into the kitchen to put one of the hens in the refrigerator and one in the freezer, I avoided eye contact. I was certain I would have started crying if our eyes met. In emotional moments, I knew my father could always see straight into my soul. I may have only known Heckle and Jeckle for a few hours, but they were my friends. Now my friends were dead.

I never considered myself a city girl. I had sense enough to know that chicken, beef, and pork didn't begin life shrink-wrapped on a Styrofoam tray in the Commissary freezer section. But after this experience, I was convinced I could never be a country girl.

The following evening, fried chicken was on the menu. I pulled a bird carcass out of the refrigerator and placed it in the sink. I looked around to make sure Mommy wasn't within earshot. She would think me silly for what I was about to say. Before I cut up the chicken, I bent over the sink.

"I swear to God, I didn't know this was going to happen," I whispered. I knew using God's name that way was absolute blasphemy, but I wanted her to know I was truly sincere. "If I had known, I would have left the side gate open, accidentally-on-purpose, and you would be free now."

Children today may have the option of refusing to eat chicken or meat of any kind. That was not an option in our family. Chicken was the least expensive protein back then. And to my mother's credit, she always found new, interesting ways to prepare it. I would have been labeled an ungrateful child for refusing the food my parents worked hard to provide.

Also, I would have starved. I know this for a fact because one time Mommy told me that when I was a child, when my father would have to bivouac or leave for a field training exercise, I would go on a hunger strike.

"What did you do?" I asked her.

"Nothing," she said.

I was shocked. "But he would be gone for days, a week sometimes."

"I know." When she realized I was staring at her in disbelief, she added, "Well, eventually he would come home and you ate again."

To make a difference in someone's life, you don't
have to be brilliant, rich, beautiful, or perfect.
You just have to care enough and be there.

~ MANDY HALE

CHAPTER 10

Ye Shall Be Known By Your Acts

Every Sunday morning when I was growing up, our family attended church services—not periodically or sporadically, but every Sunday. The only illness that would exempt us from this requirement would have been the equivalent of the Ebola virus. When Daddy was on active duty in the United States Army, we attended Protestant services on Post. When he retired from the service, we attended services at the Church of Our Savior United Methodist, a small square building just up the hill from our house in the Westwood housing division in Junction City, Kansas.

A weekly dance would occur in our home to get six people in and out of a bath and a half and dressed in time for the service at 11:00 a.m. And I mean impeccably dressed. The males wore suits and ties, the females dresses. I don't know if there is an actual verse in the Bible about presenting yourself at your best before God, but that's what my parents taught us. At twelve years old, Mommy determined I was ready to wear hosiery with my dresses. These garter stockings were the bane of my existence. Each stocking was preformed to fit a shapely woman's leg. I was neither shapely nor a woman, so the stockings would pool like deflated balloons around my ankles.

Daddy was always the first one ready—and the calmest. The rest of us rushed around like mice in a maze.

"You have ten minutes. The car is leaving in ten minutes!" Daddy called out.

I had finished getting ready and left Devereaux and Mommy jockeying for a position in front of the mirror in the upstairs bathroom. Daddy was sitting on the arm of the sofa in the living room.

"I bet you wish you were still in the Army," I told him. "Organizing troops and convoy vehicles was probably easier than wrangling these folks." Daddy winked at me and went outside to pull the car out of the garage. A few minutes later, the six of us piled into our behemoth powder-blue 1969 Ford Galaxy 500 for the ride up the hill.

Church of Our Savior United Methodist was a modest building with a sanctuary that had seating for about 100 people, but rarely saw more than fifty-five; a canteen for post-service punch and cookies, chili cook-offs and bake sales; the pastor's office; and restrooms. We arrived at the church with just enough time to greet a few folks and take our unstated, yet universally understood, reserved seats in the second row on the right side of the sanctuary.

I liked our church for many reasons. One reason was we sang a lot. Mind you, I didn't say we were good at it. No one in my family was blessed with a singing voice, but we sang our hearts out. One of my favorite hymns was "Because He Lives":

> God sent his son, they called Him Jesus;
> He came to love, heal and forgive;
> He lived and died to buy my pardon;
> An empty grave is there to prove my savior lives.
>
> Because he lives, I can face tomorrow,
> Because he lives, all fear is gone;

Because I know He holds the future,

and life is worth the living,

just because He lives.

To this day, my eyes fill with tears upon hearing this song. The hymn speaks to me because there were times in my life when I feared what tomorrow would bring. I made it through remembering that He lives.

Another reason I liked church was the length of the service: one hour. I had friends who attended other churches whose services carried on into the afternoon. They'd go home for dinner and were expected to return for an evening service.

There was no such expectation like that at Church of Our Savior United Methodist. If the pastor ran over time even ten minutes, the congregation would begin squirming in their seats. And if he repeatedly ran over time Sunday after Sunday, it would become a topic on the agenda of the next church executive board meeting. My parents impressed upon us that Christianity was as much about how you lead your life during the week—how you treated others—as it was showing up on Sunday. Long hours in church didn't automatically make you a better Christian.

One particular Sunday, when it came time for the minister's sermon, I looked down at my watch. It was 11:35. We were right on schedule. He usually spoke fifteen to twenty minutes. Then we'd bless each other in parting and be on our way. But the minister was halfway into his sermon when I realized I was no longer focusing on his words. I could hear my stomach rumbling. The preservice chaos at home rarely allowed enough time for even a bowl of cold cereal. I just prayed no one could hear the growls coming from my belly.

In our post-service tradition, my father would prepare the fluffiest, sweetest buttermilk pancakes imaginable. As I watched the minister's gestures, I could see a stack of four lovely golden-brown pancakes with creamy butter slathered between the layers, genuine maple syrup dripping down the sides from layer to layer, and four thick slices of sugar-cured bacon.

My stomach grumbled again. Mommy leaned forward in front of Devereaux and glared at me as if I could control the noise. I shrugged my shoulders.

Finally, we stood for the benediction, and I sighed. It was, however, false hope. This was when the excruciatingly painful part of Sunday morning church services began. I greeted a few people and followed Daddy out to the car. The five of us sat in the car waiting for Mommy, who seemed to think it was her mission to have a conversation with every single person in the congregation. I was an eternal optimist. I could be optimistic when there was a meal involved. I always thought each Sunday would somehow be different. But it wasn't. This was her world; we just lived in it.

Daddy checked his watch a few times. Forty-five minutes had passed. By now my stomach had a death grip on my spine.

"Come on, Bidey," I heard him say under his breath. I poked my head over the front seat.

"What was that, Daddy?" I asked.

"Nothing, I was just talking to myself," he said.

Finally, Mommy emerged talking to the pastor. We had been waiting in the car almost an hour—almost as long as the duration of the service. Everyone else had left, and the pastor was locking the front door of the church. Daddy started the engine and drove the car up to the sidewalk. Mommy got in and was a chatterbox all the way home, oblivious to how she had inconvenienced all of us.

This was a scene that repeated every Sunday. When Curtis started driving, Devereaux and I were allowed to ride to church separately with him. At least we could escape. But my father would never leave church without my mother. He never expressed anger toward her. He was an incredibly patient man.

At home, Daddy immediately headed for the kitchen. Before long, I heard the sound of sizzling bacon, and that heavenly aroma filled the house.

I went to my bedroom and changed into shorts and a T-shirt, then joined him in the kitchen.

"Buddy, can you watch the bacon for me while I change?" he asked.

"Sure." He handed me the long fork. I slid the bacon slices around the skillet to make sure they browned evenly. The hum of the exhaust fan over the stove was hypnotic. When each slice was done, I removed it from the skillet and placed it on a plate lined with paper towels to absorb the excess grease.

Daddy returned and mixed the ingredients for his pancake batter. I never saw him look at a recipe. He just knew what to add. He poured the batter into two circles on a large preheated black cast iron skillet that had been lightly coated with bacon grease. After a few seconds, bubbles started to form in the batter. Daddy noticed me watching intently.

"You see the bubbles that are forming?" he asked. I nodded. "That's part of what will make the pancakes fluffy." He picked up a metal spatula. I thought he was going to flip the pancakes. Instead, he used the spatula to lift a little bit of the outer edge of each pancake off the skillet.

"So how do you know when to flip them?" I asked.

"In a few minutes, all of the bubbles will have popped, and the surface will be dry, not shiny. That's when I'll flip them. If you do it too soon, they'll be gummy inside; leave them too long, and they'll be too dry." As Daddy explained the finer points of making the world's fluffiest pancakes to me, I remember thinking, *This man cares so much about his family that he makes pancakes for us each and every Sunday morning.*

It wasn't enough that he did these wonderful things for us. I remember one day I accompanied him while he ran errands around town. Before going home, we stopped at McDonald's for coffee. My father loved McDonald's coffee. Didn't matter what the time of day was, he was always ready for coffee.

We sat quietly in a booth as he sipped his coffee, and I licked my ice cream cone. He cleared his throat a few times and frowned slightly.

"How's that cone?' he asked.

"It's good," I said. He shifted his weight in the seat. He started to speak but then took another sip. Clearly there was something on his mind.

Finally, he said, "I realize I don't say this to you, but I love you."

"I know that, Daddy," I said slowly, unsure of the reason he felt the need to say it.

"When I was comin' up, my parents never said things like that to Garland and me." Garland was his older brother. "I want to make sure you know that."

"I do, Daddy."

He stopped and looked me directly in the eyes.

"I don't want you to ever doubt I will always be there for you."

It is only now, as an adult that I realize how difficult it was for him talk about his feelings. And though he wasn't raised that way, he was determined his own family would be different. I remember the sincere look on his face. And in the years that followed, he proved to be a man of his word.

Care about what other people think and
you will always be their prisoner.

~LAO TZU

CHAPTER 11

The Age of Aquarius

"Do you have these slacks in a size 14?" I whispered to myself as I entered the store. "Do you have these slacks in a size 14? Do you have these slacks in a size 14?" Mommy had sent me to the Montgomery Ward department store to exchange a pair of slacks. It wasn't an easy task where I could select what I wanted and head to the cash register. I needed help from a sales clerk, and for that I had to practice what I would say.

A slender woman with her hair pulled tightly in a bun and far too much powder-blue eyeshadow on her eyes greeted me as I came through the door. "May I help you?"

"Do you have these slacks in, ah, in a size 14?" My throat felt like it was likely to close halfway through the sentence, but I managed to get it out.

"I'll check for you," she said and disappeared into the racks.

Rehearsing in advance was a technique I began using as a child anytime I had to talk to a stranger. My parents trained us to stand up straight and speak clearly. But even as an adolescent, I would have to rehearse what I needed to say over and over again until I felt comfortable that I wouldn't make a fool of myself.

In junior high, I had a few friends, including Annette Leggs. While I was tall and awkward, Annette was petite and graceful. She lived a block from my house, and we hung out quite often. But when I walked down the halls in school, I tried not to make eye contact with anyone I didn't already know for fear I would have to engage in a conversation with them. I was about to finish ninth grade and start high school. The thought of starting in a new school with a new set of strangers terrified me. So when my older brother Curtis handed me a flyer about auditions for the Junction City High School (JCHS) Drill Team, I looked at him like he had lost his mind.

"What are you, nuts?" I asked him. "I can't do this."

"Of course you can," he replied.

"But I've never had dance lessons."

"They teach you the choreography."

"Curtis, I can't perform in front of people. What if I forget the steps? I'd be so embarrassed."

"You'll practice the routines enough that it will become second nature to you." For a second, I had forgotten who I was talking to. Curtis had always been active in drama club. He was incredibly talented and perfectly at home on stage. His senior year at JCHS, he was cast as the King in *The King and I*. It was a major coup for a school that typically only cast Black students in the roles of maids or janitors. He held both my shoulders and shook me gently. "You can do this, and I'll be there to help you every step of the way." And he was.

Drill team tryouts were after school in the JCHS gymnasium. The drill team sponsor, Mrs. Wynn, welcomed everyone and introduced the drill team captain and all the lieutenants. She explained these officers would perform the routine we were about to learn first. Then the officers would split us into smaller groups to break down the steps for us. The officers took their positions, and the music began. The song was "The Age of Aquarius" by The 5th Dimension.

Something happened as I watched these young women perform. I could see the delight in their faces. They weren't just executing steps; they looked like they thoroughly enjoyed what they were doing. I decided right then, this was something I had to do. Whatever issues I had about performing, I would have to overcome because this was what I wanted.

After the first session, I rushed home to Curtis to show him the steps before I forgot them. By the third session, they had given us all the steps and allowed us a few days to practice on our own before auditions. Curtis rehearsed with me in our basement over and over again until I remembered the steps well. Then he began helping me polish my performance.

"No, forget about looking at your feet. You know these steps," he said.

"Okay," I said, though less confident than he was.

"Lift your chin up. I want you to pick a spot far away, preferably beyond where the audience will be. And focus on that." I followed his instructions. "Remember your movements can't be small. You need to extend your arms and legs." I made very animated movements jokingly, but he said, "Yes, more like that."

"Really?"

"Yes, really. Think about it. You'll be performing in a gymnasium or on a football field hundreds of feet from the audience. You need to exaggerate your movements. When you pop your hip, you've got to really push it out there."

"Okay." I did it again, with more force.

"That's it! You're getting it."

On the day of the auditions, Curtis sat me down before school. "Look, I can't be there this evening." The auditions were closed. "But I want you to take a few minutes before you start your routine. Close your eyes and go over it in your mind. See yourself executing all the moves. You've done this so many times. And I know you're gonna do great."

I hugged him. "Thanks for everything."

I did as Curtis suggested. Before my turn, I envisioned myself working through the steps. When I started to perform the routine, I was, of course, nervous, but I felt comfortable on the floor. There's a point where the tempo of the music changes and starts getting funky. They sing, "Let the sunshine in . . . Let the sunshine in." By that point, my body was on autopilot. I knew my arms and legs were doing what they were supposed to. But in my heart, I felt pure joy and a level of freedom I had not experienced before. I was free from being concerned about making mistakes or what people thought of me. Free to enjoy myself.

When I finished, I knew I had done my best. I was satisfied with that. But when the results were posted, I was over-the-moon excited to see my name listed on the roster on the gymnasium door. I had earned one of only a dozen spots. I made drill team. It was the beginning of my journey toward self-confidence and priceless friendships that have lasted a lifetime.

1972

Roberta Flack wins
Record of the Year and Song of the Year
Grammy Awards for
"The First Time Ever I Saw Your Face."

CHAPTER 12

Go Blue Jays!

I was introduced to feminist ideals in junior high school. And if anyone had told me at the time that I'd ever be rockin' a pair of go-go boots and a mini skirt, I'd have said they were lying. But I set those newly discovered ideals aside for an opportunity to wear the Jay Steppers Drill Team uniform. In addition to the white go-go boots, the rest of the formal uniform was a long-sleeve mock turtleneck blue-jay-blue top with fitted bodice and a flounce skirt that ended just under the butt cheeks—with bloomers underneath, of course. Our more casual uniform was a white turtleneck under a short blue-jay-blue sleeveless jumper that had vertical slits over the legs to accentuate our kicks and a pair of blue-and-white saddle oxfords.

When we performed during football season, we would line up in order of formation about twenty minutes before the beginning of halftime. After our captain gave the command, we would march single file onto the field behind the goalpost. When we were in place, she'd yell, "Parade rest!" In response, we would stand with our legs shoulder-width apart, holding our blue-and-white pom-poms waist high behind our backs. Once at parade rest, we were not allowed to move a muscle because they did not want us to take any attention away from the game being played on the field. After all, the coaches considered us to be there as eye candy. Though we worked as hard at our craft as their players, they didn't respect us as the athletes we truly were.

Nylon stockings and those vinyl boots provided little protection from the Kansas wind that could be as cold as 10°F with the windchill factor. That twenty minutes at parade rest felt like hours some nights. I often prayed that my legs wouldn't be too stiff to move when we got the command to make our formation on the field.

It wasn't always cold, but the alternative wasn't much better. At the beginning of the season, evening temperatures were warmer. But at twilight, minute vampires flooded the humid Kansas air. I'd be standing at parade rest, unable to even flinch, while mosquitoes bit me over and over again. When I changed in the locker room after a performance, I would find drops of blood inside my boots from the mosquitoes that made a meal of my calves. No one else seemed to get bitten like that. I guess my grandmother was right. She told me some people like me are a more attractive target for bugs that bite. She said I have "sweet blood." No one can say I didn't suffer for my art.

One evening during my junior year, I was in the downstairs den with my parents. Mommy was seated at her desk, polishing her nails. Daddy was in his recliner reading the Junction City *Daily Union* newspaper—a paper he loved to read cover to cover every day. I was behind them both, lying on the couch watching television on the far side of the room.

"Well, what do we have here?" Daddy asked. He held the paper above his head so I could see a picture of the Jay Steppers Drill Team. I got up and looked over his shoulder at the newspaper. "And where are you?" It took me a minute. The picture was taken from far away, and I had to remember my position in the formation.

"There I am behind Jeanne," I said pointing.

"Here, go show this to your mama," he said, handing me the newspaper. I folded the paper over and showed the picture to my mother.

"Yeah, that's you all right," she said. Then she held up her right hand. "Do you think this nail polish color is too dark for me?" I didn't respond, knowing she didn't really care about my opinion.

"You guys should come to a game," I said.

"What do you think, Bidey?" Daddy asked.

"It'll be too cold in the stands, and I'm sure the damp air will give me a sinus headache." I looked back at Daddy who had raised both his eyebrows and bowed his head in exasperation. I got the sense he had had this conversation with my mother before.

When basketball season began, I again asked my parents about coming to a game.

"You don't have to worry about the cold," I told my mother. "It's nice and warm in the gym."

"Yes, but it will be crowded, and I'm sure all that noise will give me a headache," Mommy said. I could feel blood rushing to the top of my head. I was disappointed but also angry. I really wanted Daddy to be able to see me perform.

Because my father's personality was accommodating, it could have seemed to outsiders that my mother always had things her own way. But my father would make it clear when he reached his limit. One time, it was after an argument about the kitchen sink.

"How many times do I have to ask you to fix the kitchen sink?" my mother asked Daddy as he walked by headed for the back door. She and I were sitting at the dining room table. I had a huge tub of green beans from our backyard garden in front of me that I was snapping (removing the stem and end tip and breaking them into bite-size pieces). She was merely supervising.

Personally, I had counted seven times that she mentioned the sink in the previous two days. But if I commented, they both would have been angry with me. It was better to stay out of it. It was their battle.

"That faucet has been dripping for two weeks," she continued.

"I'll get to it when I can, Bidey," he replied. He was wearing his beat-up straw hat and denim overalls, which meant he was going to work in the yard. Daddy was methodical in the way he approached tasks around the house and rarely sat still for long.

After about half an hour, he came back inside and grabbed a soda from the refrigerator. Beads of sweat covered his entire face as he took a huge gulp. But before he could take a breath, Mommy began talking about the sink again. The barrage of words coming out of her mouth was relentless. Finally, she said, "You know that leak is just wasting water. Our water bill is high enough as it is."

"All right, all right," Daddy snapped back, throwing up his arms. "I'll go to the hardware store." He snatched the straw hat from his head and stormed off toward their bedroom. When he came back, he was tucking his wallet in the back pocket of his overalls. "I'll be back," he said, slamming the front door behind him.

Mommy continued to sit with me at the dining room table. We didn't talk. She just sat there smoking a cigarette, smiling as if she was pleased with herself.

When Daddy returned home an hour or so later, his face was more relaxed. By now, Mommy was downstairs in the laundry room. I was still at the dining room table but had moved on to peeling potatoes for dinner. He worked diligently underneath the sink for about half an hour. Then he crawled out, and when he left the kitchen, I noticed his mouth was twisted into a half-smile, which was odd since he was so angry a few hours earlier.

I approached the kitchen sink to wash the potatoes, but when I turned on the cold water tap, the water that came out burned my hands. Then I turned on the hot water tap. The water was ice cold.

Daddy had switched the lines when he installed the new fixtures, and the half-smile I witnessed earlier meant he had done it deliberately.

You little devil, I thought.

Mommy walked into the kitchen at that point, and I showed her the faucet mix-up. Her neck dropped, and she shook her head slowly.

"We need to get Daddy back here to fix this," I said.

"No, it's best to just leave it alone," she replied. She realized she had pushed her husband, the man with inexhaustible patience, one step too far.

The hot water and cold water lines in the house at 1214 Bel Air Drive remained crossed for the next ten or twelve years. To this day, when I am in a public restroom, I pause before I can remember if the hot water is supposed to be on the left side or the right.

Each time, I mutter, "Damn it, Daddy," under my breath.

In the spring of my third year in drill team, Junction City had a parade down our main street, Washington Boulevard. The Jay Steppers Drill Team was scheduled to perform. I knew this time my mother couldn't concoct an excuse not to attend. It was a community event, and her friends would have questioned why she hadn't been there to see her daughter perform.

In the staging area, we lined up in our formation. The captain gave the command, "Guide right!" We each extended our right arm to make sure we were evenly spaced from the person next to us and that our line was straight as an arrow. "Parade rest!" While I stood there waiting in formation, I could feel my chest tightening, and I had to fight hard to keep my hands from shaking behind my back. By that point, I had performed before hundreds of people. This time was different. My father would be watching.

The Blue Jay Band played our intro, and we began our routine, then started to march. I wanted to locate Daddy in the crowd, but I knew that might throw me off the routine. Instead, I focused. *Keep your back straight, knees waist-high marching. Fully extend your arms with those pom-poms.*

Touch your knee to your nose on the kicks, and for God's sake stay in line with the rest of your row.

When the parade ended, I found my parents waiting on one of the street corners.

"Well? What'd you think?" I asked.

"You were great," Daddy said, smiling ear to ear. Mommy smiled but said nothing. At the time, I was hurt that she couldn't be happy for me. I found something I enjoyed that I could do well, but she couldn't acknowledge the achievement. I thought, *How pitiful does a person have to be that their own mother won't support them?* I determined it was useless to seek her approval and remained angry with her for decades.

Looking back now, I realize that not expecting my mother's approval gave me space to develop my own identity outside the scope of her judgment. Not being under her scrutiny and constant criticism allowed me to flourish in drill team and other pursuits. They were activities that were mine and mine alone.

February 17, 1974

Richard Petty became the first driver to win
back-to-back titles at the sixteenth Daytona 500.

CHAPTER 13

"Know Your Machine"

From the time I was old enough to distinguish a pair of pliers from a socket wrench, I helped my father service and repair cars. When I was about five or six years old, my two brothers, sister, and I would go to the motor pool at Fort Riley with Daddy on off-hours. The motor pool is where the Army's vehicles and equipment were serviced.

The main building was like a huge warehouse space that had service bays lined up along each of the sidewalls. The bays were for larger vehicles that couldn't be lifted. A vehicle would be driven in over the service bay, and the mechanics would walk down a set of stairs in the bay to work on the vehicle from underneath. We had a blast climbing in and out of those bays. But the most fun were the creepers. Creepers were wooden planks about five feet by two feet and about four inches off the ground with metal wheels. The mechanic could lie on his back and push himself under a vehicle to work on it. Instead, we used them for racing. We'd team up; one person would sit on it and steer, and the other would push. We never tired of racing up and down the concrete floor of the motor pool.

We were there after-hours, so we had the run of the place, but we weren't allowed to touch any of the tools or equipment. I loved these trips because it was the only circumstance under which my mother wouldn't yell at me if I came home dirty. And if Daddy got frustrated working on a vehicle, he would openly curse. One time his hand got too close to the engine manifold, and he burned himself. "Son of a bitch," he shouted and tossed the tool he was using on the floor. "Hot dammit" and "shit" periodically escaped his lips as well. This was such a departure from his usual even-tempered disposition that it surprised me at first. But the more often I heard it, the more it made me giggle. It was funny as hell to hear Daddy swear.

When I was a junior in high school, Daddy bought me a 1961 Plymouth Valiant at a police auction for the weighty sum of $100. The car was in decent shape for being eleven years old, but its best feature was its super cool push-button gears.

On one occasion, Daddy and I were performing a tune-up on my Valiant. At that time, he had already retired from the United States Army. He was an auto mechanics instructor for the vocational technical school on Post, preparing soldiers for jobs in the civilian workplace, so he still had access to the motor pool.

Daddy had enlisted the help of a welding instructor to build the tool racks he used in his classes. Each tool rack was a four-foot-by-four-foot square wooden board mounted at an angle on a rolling stand. Tools were displayed on hooks on the board. The especially clever part was that when you removed a tool from the rack, a red shadow in the shape of the tool showed on the board. That way you knew exactly where to replace the tool. It was a great way to inventory the tools, but more importantly, it was a safety check. A lot of damage could be done to the car or the mechanic if an engine was started with a stray tool under the hood.

Daddy wheeled the tool tray to the side of my car. He raised the hood and began removing the spark plugs with a socket wrench. When he had removed all six, he handed them to me and said, "Buddy, could you clean these for me?"

"Sure," I said.

"And set the points to . . ." He paused to check the spec sheet. "Set the points to .02."

"Got it," I said.

The firing end of each spark plug had a metal hook. I placed the hook of the spark plug into the cleaner and turned on the air compressor. The machine sandblasted corrosion off the hook. Once all the spark plugs were clean, I slid the spark plug gauge—a metal disc surrounded by spokes of varying thicknesses—under the hook to determine the size of the gap between the hook and the plug. If the space was too wide or too narrow, the spark plug wouldn't deliver the proper electrical charge, and the engine could sputter or possibly stall. I used the metal loop on the gauge to adjust each spark plug to the specification Daddy gave me.

When I finished the last spark plug, I proudly placed them on a rag on the car's fender. Daddy pulled his head from under the hood, inspected my work, and said, "Good job." I stood up straighter and smiled. "You can check your tire pressure next if you want."

"Okay," I said. I picked up a tire gauge from the board. I pulled the air hose out and dragged it around the car to reach the farthest tire. I then stepped on the hose so it wouldn't retract back into the wall socket. I removed the cap from the tire and measured the pressure with the gauge. It needed another five pounds of pressure, so I attached the air hose and released the air. I measured the tire pressure a second time. It was good, so I moved on to the next tire. As I worked my way around the car, I thought of how much I enjoyed learning from Daddy. Cooking lessons with my mother were a totally different experience.

According to my mother, my potatoes were always too runny or too stiff; my vegetables were always overcooked or undercooked; and my meat was always too salty or not seasoned enough. The advantage of working with Daddy versus my mother was Daddy always encouraged me. Even if he had to correct my work, he did it in a respectful way. My mother, on the other hand, only criticized. She never once told me, "Good job."

Not once.

My father always impressed upon me the importance of using my senses to "know" my machine. He would pull up to a stoplight, nod toward the car next to us, and say something like, "That lady's bearings are shot," or "his chassis needs to be lubed."

One time, he and I had returned from a trip to Milleson Auto Supply— his favorite hangout. He pulled into the driveway of our home and stopped the car before going into the garage. He frowned and tilted his head.

"Listen, you hear that?" he asked. I listened but didn't detect a thing.

"Hear what?" I responded.

"That noise." I still didn't hear anything, so I frowned and tilted my head as he had done, hoping that would help. After a few seconds, I looked back up at him. Daddy flashed his 75-watt smile at me.

"You're messing with me. There's no noise."

"Gotcha," he said. He poked me in the side and started tickling me.

My father wanted me to understand about cars because he knew women are more likely than men to be the target of unscrupulous mechanics. His lessons were sometimes self-serving though. He once told me a clean car runs better. He got plenty of free car washes out of me before I realized that was a bogus one. He also told me a car runs better on a "full belly." That had a practical purpose. When I learned to drive in the 1970s, America was in the middle of an energy crisis. A shortage of crude oil caused long lines at the gas station. He wanted me to always keep my gas tank more than half full because we never knew when the gas supply would run out.

As an homage to my father, I have kept every car I owned in peak running condition. In 1997, I bought a brand new six-cylinder deep violet Ford Mustang. Ford made very few Mustangs in that glorious shade of purple. As much as I love the throaty sound of an eight-cylinder Mustang Cobra engine, I opted for the six instead. I have only received one speeding ticket in my life. I knew I'd be getting popped once a month if I had a Cobra.

The following year, my parents came to visit me in California. Daddy had just finished restoring an eight-cylinder 1968 Mustang to its original condition. When he saw mine, he beamed and said, "My, my, my, isn't that a beautiful sight?" I, of course, had to take him for a test drive. When we turned toward the on-ramp, I floored the accelerator. As we flew up onto the freeway, I turned to Daddy and said, "It's not an eight, but this puppy still can move." Daddy burst out laughing.

I drove my beautiful Mustang for sixteen years, and I reached a point where I didn't have to look at the mileage to know when it was due for an oil change. I could tell by the smell coming from the engine.

With all the computer systems in modern cars, the most maintenance I can do is fill the windshield washer fluid. And I hate it when daylight savings time rolls around. I have to consult the manual of my 2016 Subaru Forester to change the dashboard clock. After paging through multiple menus, and after twenty minutes have passed, I finally get to the right screen to change the time. I can hear my father's voice in my head: "Cynthia, you've got to know your machine."

Friendship is the hardest thing in the world to explain. It's not something you learn in school. But if you haven't learned the meaning of friendship, you really haven't learned anything.

~MUHAMMAD ALI

CHAPTER 14

Magnificent 7: The Early Years

By my senior year of high school, I had become close friends through drill team with Jeanne Williams, Denise Madkins, Charlotte Jackson, Marsha Slaughter, and Gwen Macon. And though my friend Annette Leggs wasn't on drill team, she was always there to cheer us on.

Denise was a natural beauty. When other girls were spending time at the bathroom mirror laboriously applying makeup, Denise would swipe each eye with mascara and keep going. Charlotte had an enviable hourglass figure, and I admired her ability to get to the point. She spoke honestly about how things were without hurting people's feelings. Jeanne had a petite frame and boundless energy. I have never been a morning person, but Jeanne would greet me with a bright smile and my day just seemed to start better. Marsha had long black hair, a slim figure, and was a great dancer. I also loved to hear her laugh. Gwen was our school drill team captain and a great instructor. She choreographed a lot of our dance routines, and whenever we performed, I would always look to her if I got out of step. Annette had a wry sense of humor that always cracked me up. We looked like an odd pair together, as she had a petite frame, and I am tall and used to be very thin. My friends were all pretty on the outside, but each of them also had good hearts and were always willing to help others.

Every Saturday morning during high school, we each watched *Soul Train* on television. It was the self-proclaimed "hippest trip in America!" Later that night we would try the new moves we learned from *Soul Train* when we danced at the Non Commissioned Officers (NCO) Club on Post. The guy-to-girl ration at the NCO Club was probably as much as five to one, so there was no shortage of dance partners.

When I think of it now, I am surprised my parents let me go to the NCO Club. Most of the men we interacted with were in their midtwenties to forty-plus. But because the club was on Post, these men knew they'd better be on their best behavior. Otherwise, it could affect their United States Army career.

We looked out for each other when we were clubbing. Someone would always stay behind to watch purses and make sure no one spiked our drinks. And before we left the club, we counted off in birth order—Gwen, Jeanne, Marsha, Denise, Annette and me (born the same day), and Charlotte—to make sure no one was left behind. Decades later we would call ourselves the Magnificent 7 or Mag 7, like the western movie from the 1960s.

We lived in a community that was culturally diverse because of Fort Riley. Even among my friends, all our fathers were Black, and Gwen, Marsha, and I had Black mothers. But Charlotte's and Denise's mothers were from Germany, and Annette's and Jeanne's mothers were from Korea. While diversity was present in our community, it was not typical for the rest of the state of Kansas, which was predominantly white. When Jay Steppers Drill Team traveled to other cities to compete, we were successful because we were good dancers. Also, our leader Mrs. Wynn allowed us to perform to music we enjoyed. We had a killer routine to the hottest song at the time, Isaac Hayes's "Theme from Shaft."

Whether traveling to compete with other drill teams or perform at out-of-town sports games, we didn't always receive a friendly welcome. Our athletes were some of the best in the state, and their talents weren't always appreciated in the towns we visited. In the 1970s there were still bridges that had "Nigger Don't Let the Sun Set on You" painted on them. Quite a few times, after we were loaded back on the buses ready to return home, we would hear shouts like, "Nigger go home," or "Monkeys go back to Africa," by students from other high schools.

The students weren't brave enough to say those things to our faces. They knew we could beat them in football, basketball, *and* wrestling. Therefore, we sure as hell could beat the shit out of them in the parking lot.

I never thought much of the comments at the time. I considered the slurs to be rantings of the ignorant. As Blacks, we were a small percentage of the thirty-six-member drill team, and none of the other girls on the squad treated us any differently. Having to guard against ignorance from the out-of-towners may have been part of what made my Mag 7 friends and I closer. We weren't going to let people treat us as "other than."

Many talents and personalities are represented in our group. We have an eternal optimist, a cautious pessimist, a dreamer, a visionary, a wry humorist, a pragmatist, and a guardian who holds the bail money and makes sure everyone is taken care of. In Mag 7 we acknowledge and celebrate our differences. At a time when I dealt with a mother who criticized my every move, these young women accepted me with all my flaws and failings and never tried to change me. It means the world to me that they are still my good friends after fifty-plus years.

There is nothing noble in being superior to your fellow man; true nobility is being superior to your former self.

~EARNEST HEMINGWAY

CHAPTER 15
The Aptitude Test

After high school, I was accepted at Kansas State University (K-State) in Manhattan, Kansas. By my junior year in 1977, I had settled into the rhythm of college life. I lived in Moore Hall, a coed dormitory, and was satisfied with cafeteria food, but it was always good to have a supply of snacks—or brain food as I liked to call it—available in my room for late-night studying. My supply was running low, so I decided to make a run to my parents' house twenty miles away in Junction City. By this time, both my sister Devereux and I were at Kansas State University; my brother Curtis was in law school at Kansas University in Lawrence, Kansas; and my brother Cyril had been serving in the United States Navy for several years. Yet, my mother still stocked the downstairs pantry as if six people lived there.

After a thirty-minute drive, I arrived at the house in the early evening. A familiar aroma greeted me as I walked into the house. My mother sat at the dining room table shelling peas. Her even-toned chestnut-brown complexion never needed foundation. The sides of my mother's prematurely silver and black hair were smoothed back and secured in a French twist, as a wavy stream of curls graced the top of her head. She was dressed in a sleeveless blouse with slacks. A lit cigarette, her constant companion at the time, lay smoldering in an ashtray beside her.

"Hi, Mommy," I said. Her almond-shaped eyes brightened when she saw me.

"Well, hello," she said. As I moved toward her, her eyes surveyed my appearance. I no longer pressed my hair and was sporting an afro, but I knew that wasn't what she was looking at. I was wearing a T-shirt, denim jacket, and faded blue jeans that were flared and frayed at the bottom. The disapproval was evident on her face. Mommy never thought blue jeans were appropriate attire for a proper young lady. Decades later she explained to me why she hated me wearing denim.

My parents were raised on farms in Arkansas in the 1930s. During the Depression, white farmers drove by farms owned by Black people and tossed old clothes, mostly faded blue jeans and overalls full of holes, to the Black farmers. Though the white farmers were as poor as the Black ones, they acted superior by giving their cast-offs to the Black farmers. For Mommy, denim was a painful symbol of poverty and racism.

When I was a college student, blue jeans were my school uniform. Had I known about the cast-offs at the time, I would not have worn my tattered blue jeans or overalls in my mother's presence.

Mommy shook her head as if to accept she could no longer control how I dressed and went back to shelling peas.

"Don't tell me," I said and inhaled deeply. "You made smothered steak for dinner, right?" My mother would pound steak until it was thin, batter and fry it, then smother it in an incredibly flavorful gravy.

"Yes," she laughed. "There's leftovers in the refrigerator if you want some."

"No thanks. I'm just here for a few things. I've got to get back."

Mommy understood. She worried about me driving at night. The quickest route back to the university was Interstate 70 to Kansas Highway

18. I-70 was okay, but there were no lights on K-18—just miles of farmland with no houses in sight.

"I got that hot chocolate you like. And there was a sale on deodorant. Help yourself."

I jumped down the basement stairs two at a time, proud of the skill I had mastered after so many years in the house. My father was sitting in his recliner in the den with his back to me. He had a makeshift writing board—a three-foot-by-two-foot piece of plywood—in front of him resting on the arms of the chair. Several workbooks were stacked to his right. Another stack of workbooks was on the floor to the left of his chair. I ran my hand over his curly salt-and-pepper hair.

"Hey, Daddy," I said. He looked up and grinned at me with teeth that shone bright against his dark complexion. Black-framed United-States-Army-issued glasses rested on his nose. Though he was retired from the military, he saw no need to change his glasses in the interest of fashion. He wore a plain V-neck white T-shirt, khaki slacks, and corduroy house slippers. I leaned over the chair, and the familiar scent of Old Spice aftershave greeted my nostrils.

"Hey, fella, when did you get here?" The stubble from his five o'clock shadow tickled as he kissed my cheek.

"A few minutes ago. I'm on a turnaround trip. Just need a few supplies."

"Okay."

I walked back to the pantry. The washer and dryer were on the left wall, and Mommy's clotheslines sloped from the edges of the ceiling. The far wall had floor to ceiling shelves with bulky items on the bottom row, smaller items at the top. I smiled when I saw the deodorant. She had bought a twelve-pack. I grabbed two and tossed some snacks in brown paper bags: potato chips, Ritz crackers, pretzels, Cheetos, hot chocolate, apple cider, paper cups and plates, plastic silverware, shampoo, Irish Spring bar soap, body lotion, and Crest toothpaste.

When I finished checking everything off my shopping list, I put the two sacks at the bottom of the stairs and joined Daddy in the den. I sat down next to him, where the student workbooks he had finished grading were stacked on the floor. After my father retired from the service, he was hired to teach auto mechanics to juniors and seniors at Junction City High School.

Curious to know how much I remembered of what Daddy taught me about cars growing up, I picked up one of the workbooks he had already graded. Flipping through the pages, I stopped on a cross-section illustration of a car engine. I covered the answers with my hand and said the names of each of the engine parts quietly so I wouldn't distract Daddy as he continued grading. When I lifted my hand and saw I had named nine of the ten parts correctly, I was delighted.

As I continued to flip pages, a loose piece of paper fell to the floor. The paper's edges were worn. It had been folded and unfolded so many times the creases were worn. The text had been duplicated multiple times too—so much so that the typeface was fuzzy in spots. When I reached down to pick up the paper, I read the title.

"NIGGER APTITUDE TEST" was written across the top of the page.

"What the . . ." I said, stopping short of expressing the words in my head because I didn't cuss in front of my parents. I continued to read as I picked up the paper. There were a series of questions, including:

How many coons does it take to fill up a row boat?

How much watermelon can you eat in fifteen minutes?

How many dead niggers can hang from a poplar without breaking the tree's limbs?

By now my heart was racing, and the top of my ears were burning.

"Daddy," I said slowly. With an outstretched arm, I held up the paper between two fingers and turned it toward him. "What is this?"

"It's a page Jimmy stuck in the back of his workbook." He finished another workbook, closed it, and placed it on the pile.

"And let me guess, Jimmy is white?"

"Yes."

"I don't believe this. So he knew you'd see it when you graded his book?" Daddy nodded and continued with his work.

"I realize we live in Kansas, but this is the 1970s for goodness' sake. It is outrageous. What are you going to do about it?"

"What is there to do?" He looked up at me over his glasses, his eyebrows lifted and his eyes wide.

"Surely you'll have a talk with this Jimmy person, right?" Now not just my ears were burning; my whole head felt like it was on fire. I was angry with Jimmy for disrespecting my father but also angry he didn't see the colossal insult the paper represented.

"What's there to talk about?"

"This is absolutely offensive. He's being disrespectful to you."

"That may have been his intention." I sat there with my mouth open in disbelief. After an awkward silence, he stopped grading, laid down his pen, and looked up at me again. "There is nothing on that page but a bunch of racist stereotypes that have nothing to do with me. All Jimmy has done is show his own ignorance. He put it in his workbook to get a rise out of me." He smiled and waved his hand away. "I wouldn't give him the satisfaction." He shrugged his shoulders and went back to grading. "I will continue to treat him with respect like I do all my students, even if I don't get respect in return. That's who I am."

I didn't understand why Daddy didn't share my outrage. A part of my brain was raging now. I wanted to stay overnight and march into Daddy's classroom the next morning and slap the shit out of Jimmy. I could see the headlines in the Junction City *Daily Union* newspaper: "Twenty-Year-Old College Student Assaults Senior High Schooler." I shook my head to get rid of the violent thoughts. I was frustrated I wasn't getting my point across. But continuing the conversation would have ended in an argument.

"Better you than me, Daddy. Better you than me," I said. I kissed his cheek, grabbed my bags, and headed upstairs much slower than I'd come down. Mommy frowned when she saw the confusion on my face.

"What's wrong?" she asked.

"I, um," I said. I realized it would have taken too long to explain, and I wasn't sure how to describe what just happened anyway, so I just threw up my hands. "Just ask Daddy" was all I could manage. "Take care, and I'll see ya in a couple of weeks." She blinked a few times.

"Sure, you drive safe now."

Only after I made the transition from I-70 to K-18, when there was only darkness and quiet and disappearing white lines in the road, did I begin to comprehend my father's reaction. Daddy was raised under Jim Crow laws in the South. He joined a segregated United States Army in 1947 and served during the integration of the service and through the 1960s. He had dealt with racists far more insidious than Jimmy during his career and lifetime.

That night Daddy taught me a valuable lesson. I can't control how people in this world try to treat me, but I can absolutely choose what my response will be. The wisdom he shared with me that night served me well throughout my professional career and in my personal life.

According to census statistics, the number of Blacks attending college rose from 282,000 in 1966 to 1,062,000 in 1976—an increase of 275 percent. In addition . . . only about 39 percent of Blacks who go to college for a year eventually graduate, compared to a 57 percent graduation rate for whites.

~LAWRENCE FEINBERG AND JUAN WILLIAMS, EXCERPT FROM "NUMBER OF BLACKS IN COLLEGE TRIPLES IN PAST DECADE," *The Washington Post*, JUNE 10, 1978

CHAPTER 16
Enter M.P.

In my first few years at K-State, I dated a few times but not enough to consider myself in a relationship. That is, until I met a man named M.P., or at least that's what I called him. It was the summer before I was to begin my senior year at K-State. Soon I would graduate with a bachelor's degree in political science/prelaw. A friend and I had been dancing at the NCO Club on Post at Fort Riley one Saturday night, and we stopped at a coffee shop in Junction City before going home. M.P. was a few inches taller than me at five foot, nine inches, with a dark complexion and eyes that sparkled when he smiled. As a former Golden Gloves boxing champion, his build was muscular. He had a quick wit and could make me smile regardless of my mood.

When the fall semester began, my good friend Valerie and I moved into an attractive apartment complex that was a short walk from campus. She and I met as freshmen, and after pledging Delta Sigma Theta Public Service Sorority together in the spring of 1976, we became inseparable. Valerie was intelligent, funny, kind, and considerate. Reddish-brown hair framed her flawless light-skinned complexion. Always fashionably dressed, she had looks that turned all the men's heads. This was the first time each of us experienced the freedom of living outside the dormitories. The arrangement suited us both. We thoroughly enjoyed our lives.

M.P. and I began spending more and more time together. He was a military police officer (M.P.) assigned to the brig (jail) at Fort Riley. That's why I refer to him as M.P. Our schedules only allowed us to be together evenings and some weekends, depending on his duty assignments. As a result, he would often sleep overnight at my apartment.

My parents had instilled in me that premarital sex was an unforgiveable sin. Therefore, I made it crystal clear to M.P. that I had no intention of going to hell, so the nights he stayed over, we only cuddled.

I was attracted to M.P. because of his sweet personality. Like my college friends, he called me Doss and had a way of saying my name that made me melt. He brought me flowers, jewelry, and other gifts. He was physically affectionate and constantly told me how beautiful and sexy I was. No man had ever said those things to me before. Twenty-one-year-old me was flattered.

My courses were interesting, and school was going along nicely. Valerie and I enjoyed rooming together. We were compatible as roommates. But the apartment complex we had chosen proved to be very expensive. By November, we realized we would have to make other arrangements.

"This is not good," I told M.P. one evening. "It's the middle of the school year. Most apartments are under contract for a year. All the good apartments will be leased until spring."

"Maybe you can move back into the dorm," M. P. suggested.

"Nah, I don't think so," I said. My experience with roommates assigned by the housing authority in the dorm always ended in disaster. Over the previous three years in the dorm, I had a parade of roommates, all of them white, all of them from tiny Kansas towns. None of them had ever met a Black person before, let alone shared a living space with one. The tension in the air from the condescension and distrust was palpable. One roommate spoke to me the day she moved in and said nothing else to me. I returned from class one afternoon, and all her belongings were gone. She didn't even last a week.

I was not interested in living in another hostile environment. "But I don't see how I am going to find a decent place in the middle of the school year."

"Don't worry, Doss," M.P., ever the ray of sunshine, said. "You'll find something."

"And what do I do with my things. When we vacate this place, I'll have to take all of my stuff to Junction City, only to bring it back in a few weeks for the new semester."

"No, you won't," he said. "Anything you don't want to take home, you'll leave with me until you get your new place." M.P. rented a small house in Manhattan with a few of his Army buddies. I smiled and kissed him.

"You are so sweet," I said, turning my back to him. I nuzzled against his chest as he wrapped his arms around me.

The following weekend, I moved some small furniture pieces and a few boxes to M.P.'s place and began searching for a new apartment. After two weeks of searching, I finally found a small one-bedroom basement apartment that was within my budget. Though it was a lot farther away from campus, I felt lucky something was even available.

Valerie found a tiny studio apartment. I was sad she and I would no longer be living together. We slogged through three years in the dorms. Our senior year was the time to enjoy ourselves. The more overwhelmed I felt with the changes, the more M.P. inserted himself into my life. While I prepared for finals, M.P. brought me meals, ran errands for me, and massaged my neck after long study sessions. But he was so intense. When we were together, he always had his arms around me, smothering me with kisses. He talked a lot about our future and how he wanted a family, and while I knew I probably wanted children someday, I wasn't thinking that far into the future. I was focused on finishing my last year of college, getting my bachelor's degree, and starting law school.

One morning I awoke and felt a searing pain in my pelvis. At first, I thought it was menstrual cramps, but because I wasn't due for another week, I dismissed the idea. I was still groggy from sleep, but as I became more awake, I realized M.P. was on top of me. I was lying on my stomach, and the weight of his body made it hard for me to breathe. I was shocked when I realized his penis was inside me.

"What are you doing?" I cried. "Get off me!" With all my strength, I tried to push up, but my arms were like spaghetti. His muscular build was too much for me. He didn't budge. Finally, after a few minutes of struggling, he let out a guttural moan, removed his limp penis, and rolled off of me. I got out of bed.

"You were lying there," he said. "Your body is just so sexy. I couldn't help myself."

"Have you lost your mind?" I yelled. "Get out!"

He continued to try to talk, but I was so outraged I ignored his words. Finally, he collected his belongings and left.

I stood there shaking, not wanting to believe what had just happened. I immediately ran into the shower, needing to rid myself of his smell. I stood under the hot water and scrubbed my skin, but I couldn't wash away the pain in my vagina—the remaining evidence. Otherwise I could pretend like the assault didn't happen. And that's how I thought of it: as an assault. It would be many years before I could admit to myself that it was rape. Rape was too intimate and personal. Even more painful was the realization I had been betrayed by a man I trusted.

After I showered, I dressed and got ready to go to class. The Kansas wind was brutal that day. Or maybe it was just that I felt so vulnerable. It was as if my body was a sieve. I sat through my classes but had little retention of what the instructors said. I was determined not to allow the rape to affect me. I felt that if it did, it meant he won.

M.P. called several times a day, but I allowed the answering machine to pick up. He left messages begging me to forgive him. Sometimes he'd say he just wanted to talk with me so he could explain himself, but other times he left angry messages calling me a bitch for not talking to him.

It was a good thing the semester break came quickly. Going home to Junction City, putting some distance between us was just what I needed. I expected him to try to call me at my parents' house but knew he wasn't stupid enough to show up on their doorstep. Not after what he'd done. I told my parents M.P. and I had broken up, and I didn't want to speak to him if he called but didn't say more than that.

One afternoon, my parents were at work, and I answered the phone without thinking.

"Doss residence, Cynthia speaking." It was the way our parents had trained us to respond as children.

"Doss, it's me. We need to talk," M.P. said, trying to sound like his previous sweet self.

"I have nothing left to say to you."

"But I have your stuff."

Shit! I thought. *I had totally forgotten.* "My new lease begins the first of January. Can I pick it up from you next Saturday?" I asked as if this was a business transaction.

"Okay, what time?"

"Noon should work, but I'll have to double-check with Daddy."

"You're bringing your father?" The sweetness had left his voice.

"Yeah, we'll load it all in his truck. That way we'll only have to make one trip."

"Oh."

"I'll let you know if anything changes. Bye." A shudder went through my body. Talking to M.P., hearing his voice again made me want to take a shower.

On Saturday, the first thing I saw when Daddy and I rounded the corner of M.P.'s street was my belongings piled in the middle of his front yard surrounded by at least a foot and a half of snow.

"What the . . .?" Daddy stopped short of cursing. He pulled into the driveway behind M.P.'s car. He got out and headed for the porch.

"Daddy, we don't need him. Unfortunately, it looks like everything is out here," I said. Everything was there all right, and from the condition of some of the boxes, had been sitting there in the snow for several hours. Daddy acted like he didn't hear me and was now banging on the screen door, calling M.P.'s name.

I started moving boxes into the truck bed, and Daddy joined me after he realized M.P. was not going to show himself. After stowing a half-dozen or so boxes in the truck, my body began shivering. It was, after all, barely 2°F outside. Daddy tossed me the truck keys.

"You go warm up in the truck, buddy," he said. "I can finish this."

I would have continued to help, especially since I felt I created this mess, but was thankful for the truck's heater. Daddy stowed the furniture pieces and was carrying the final box to the truck when he turned on his heel and shouted back at the house. "What kind of man are you?" He started to the truck again but turned back once more and said, "That's just it—you're not a man!" He threw the last box into the truck bed and slammed the tailgate shut. The whole time I could see he was muttering something to himself. But even after he jumped into the cab, I couldn't understand him. His jaw was clenched, and he thrust the gearshift on the steering wheel up so hard I thought it would snap off. We reversed out of the driveway and were on the road for a few minutes before he reached over and patted my knee. "You okay, buddy?"

"Yes, sir. I'm fine." And I wanted to ask him, "But are you okay?" I had never seen my father that angry before. I was glad M.P. hadn't come to the door because I didn't know what Daddy would have done to him.

Do what you feel in your heart to be right
– for you'll be criticized anyway.

~ELEANOR ROOSEVELT

CHAPTER 17

Who Gets to Choose?

"Doss, I know you're in there," I heard M.P. yell. "Please talk to me. I know I messed up, but you have to talk to me."

Two feet of snow was on the ground, but that didn't deter him from standing at the door of my basement apartment for at least half an hour trying to get me to come upstairs. My apartment had a small kitchen, full bath, living room, and bedroom. It suited my needs, but there were no frills. I was lucky to find it in the middle of the school year. I lay on the couch of my dank, dark apartment with a pillow over my ears trying to drown out the sound of his voice. I kept my previous phone number, so my friends could reach me. It never occurred to me he would be able to find my new address from the phone listing. M.P.'s behavior scared me. I didn't know what he would do next. I only left my apartment when absolutely necessary for fear I would run into him. I was furious he made me a prisoner in my own home.

One morning I got up and felt sick to my stomach. When I stood up, the room started spinning, and I broke out in a cold sweat. January was flu season, so I went to the student health center.

The doctor, an attractive man in his early thirties with a very compassionate bedside manner, asked me, "Could you be pregnant?" I shook my head at the thought. *The world couldn't possibly be that cruel.*

"I don't think so," I replied, twirling a ring on my right finger. They ran some tests, and while I waited for the results, I never considered I was dealing with anything more than the flu. I thought I'd just walk out with a prescription for an antibiotic.

Instead, the doctor told me, "You're pregnant." It felt like a blade pierced my heart. My limbs were numb as if all the blood had drained from them. "If you decide to have the baby, I'll prescribe some prenatal vitamins for you, and I have some brochures on adoption I can give you. If not, I can refer you to a clinic. I know this is a lot for you to absorb, but I want you to know you have options," he said. "You don't have to decide now. Take some time and think about it."

I didn't tell the doctor, but I was pretty certain I knew what I had to do. It was just six years after the landmark United States Supreme Court case Roe v. Wade upheld the fundamental right to privacy, which protects a pregnant woman's right to an abortion.

If I had a baby, I would have to postpone finishing my degree, and it would be impossible to go to law school. I came from a small town that didn't offer good job opportunities. The most I could expect would be a minimum wage position. I considered what it would be like to raise a child as a single parent with no money. Adoption was out of the question; I couldn't imagine having a child of mine raised by someone else. No, I could not have a baby. More importantly, I could not have M.P.'s baby.

The next time M.P. called, I answered the phone.

"I'm pregnant" was all I said.

"I know."

"What do you mean you know?"

"Well, I had my suspicions. Doss, I tracked your periods, and I guessed when you'd be ovulating. You said you wanted to have a family while you were young. This is a blessing. The two of us are going to be parents."

I could not believe what I was hearing. He timed the rape with the intention of making me pregnant. As though a child would prevent me from leaving him. If I had any doubts about my decision, they disintegrated completely after hearing M.P.'s admission. I realized how delusional he was. He lived in a twisted universe if he thought his behavior was acceptable. Every kindness, every expression of affection, all the gifts were part of a deliberate plan to hijack my life. I knew I needed to get as far away from him as possible.

"How dare you make that decision for me! You had no right."

"I want us to have a future together. Doss, you'll be finishing school soon, and I've never been to college. I know you'll be starting your career, so where does that leave me? All those things I told you about my family weren't true. My father doesn't own a liquor store. He's just a clerk there. I said that to impress you. I was afraid of losing you."

Now I was furious. I never cared about what his father did for a living, and I was insulted and angry he thought I was so shallow as to believe a clerk's son was not good enough for me.

"Your plan was wrong on so many levels, and in the end, it didn't work. I'm not having the baby. There's a clinic where I can have an abortion."

"Doss, you can't."

"I can and I will. Goodbye, M.P."

I sat on my couch staring at the wall on the other side of my living room. I have no idea how long I remained there after hanging up the phone. This life that M.P. imagined for the two of us was all in his head. The fact that he would go to such lengths to manipulate me without understanding the lunacy of what he had done terrified me.

He continued to call several times a day and came by my apartment trying to get me to talk to him. I was lucky my landlord didn't live on-site because M.P. created such a disturbance at my door, and I could have gotten evicted. I never responded to his calls or answered the door. I had nothing left to say to him. He was a liar, a manipulator . . . a rapist.

There is no greater agony than bearing
an untold truth inside you.

~MAYA ANGELOU

CHAPTER 18

I Will Survive

At times, I was confident I wouldn't let my predicament ruin my life, but there were also times when I would curl up on my couch, unable to do anything or go anywhere. When I did make it to campus, I would pass groups of people and imagine they were talking about me. The slightest noise would make me jump, and I seemed to always be cold. On the way to my biology class, I had to pass a display in the hallway. About a dozen gallon jars lined the walls, each holding preserved fetuses in different stages of development. I had always found the display disturbing. It lacked dignity, like something in a carnival freak show. Now that I was pregnant, I was incensed by it.

If I were going to have a child, it would need to be on my terms. I would need to be established in my career and married in a committed, stable relationship with the father, a compassionate man who shared my commitment to providing a loving, secure environment for our children. M.P. was not the man I envisioned as the father of my children.

That man would be like my father—a man who put others' needs ahead of his own. Daddy was even-tempered and never held a grudge. If he got mad at me for something I did, it didn't last long. He had an infinite capacity to forgive people and let go of the past. He was a caring man, fiercely protective of his family. If I had a problem, I knew I could count on him to listen and provide sound guidance.

It was natural that I would want to talk to him first. A week had passed since receiving the test results. I chose a Saturday morning to call because I knew Mommy would be at the Commissary on Post shopping for hours. The tiny windows of my basement apartment allowed only limited light in. Sitting on the couch, I looked around my living room. I had a knack for decorating on a budget, but I knew I would only be in the apartment a few months, so I hadn't bothered.

I did, however, manage to put up two butterfly prints on canvas that hung on the living room wall opposite me on the couch. I have always studied and admired butterflies—how simple caterpillars turn into raving beauties with vibrant color combinations. I also admired their freedom. They bob and weave through the air as if changing their minds which flower to feed on mid-flight. But freedom was the opposite of how I felt that night. Instead, I felt trapped by circumstances I didn't believe I deserved.

I dialed the first few numbers on my rotary phone and then hung up. I did this several times. My shoulders were hunched over as my stomach churned, and I had a bitter taste in my mouth. Finally, I took a deep breath and completed the number.

"Hi, Daddy. It's me."

"Hey, buddy," he said. "How are you?"

"Not so good."

"Are you having trouble with your classes?"

"No, well, yes. Biology is kicking my butt. I've got an exam next week. But that's not what I mean."

"What's wrong?"

There was silence as I gathered my thoughts and tried to form the right words in my head. How could I tell him I had failed to safeguard my virtue, one of the most important rules my parents taught me? It didn't matter I had been raped; I felt I never should have trusted M.P. I should have known he was devious. I would rather my parents think I had been careless than admit a man outsmarted me. The logic of my thinking at the time is not relevant to me today. It wasn't until decades later that I realized it was not about being outsmarted. M.P. was an abusive manipulator who had given me no reason *not* to trust him. He was, by all appearances, a sweet, passionate man. I had done nothing wrong.

Still, that night, sitting in my apartment while my father waited for my response, the words swelled in my throat. I heard the Westminster chime of the German mantle clock striking the half hour in the background, a sound that normally soothed me; instead, it made me cry.

"Ah, come on now, buddy," he said. "Don't cry. Tell me what's wrong." His voice was as calm and soothing as always.

When I finished sobbing, I said, "Daddy, I'm pregnant." I wrapped the phone cord around my index finger in the silence that followed.

"Who's the father, M.P.?"

"Yes, sir. And Daddy, ever since I broke up with him, he's been coming by my apartment banging on the door trying to get me to come out. Sometimes he leaves messages on my answering machine calling me nasty names. Then other times, he says how much he loves me and wants me back. I don't think he's mentally stable, and I certainly don't think he's suitable to be a good father. How can I raise a child with a father who's unstable?" *And not to mention a rapist.*

"Well, ultimately, it's your decision. I trust your judgment, and I'm here to help you whatever you decide," Daddy said. "But we have to tell your mother now."

"I know, but I'm a mess. Let me call you guys tomorrow."

My father always knew the right words to say. After talking to him, my shoulders felt lighter. I sat up straighter with my chest open, but I couldn't relax yet. I needed to prepare to break the news to my mother. I knew her first response would be how this news would reflect on *her*. I couldn't cry like I did with my father.

The following day with both my parents on the phone, I told my mother the news. I had rehearsed every word so my voice would be even. I even paced up and down my living room floor so my body wouldn't shake from nervousness. Facing the prospect of having an abortion was scary, but having to tell my mother I was pregnant was the hardest thing I had ever done.

Her first question was, "Who all knows about this?"

"Only M.P. and my friend Valerie know," I said. "No one else."

"Let's keep it that way. What are you going to do?"

"Student Health gave me a referral to an abortion clinic in Kansas City."

It didn't surprise me that my mother didn't ask how I was doing, but that didn't mean it hurt any less. I felt a throbbing pain in my chest. She must have known I was scared, that I could have used some reassuring words. She was more concerned about whether her friends would find out about the pregnancy and chose to speak to me without compassion or sympathy.

I never told my parents the full story of what happened to me—that a devious man had abused me. After seeing Daddy's anger the day we picked up my belongings from M.P.'s house, I didn't know what he might do to M.P. And I certainly didn't want him getting in trouble because of me.

On February 6, 1979, at 7:40 a.m. at a clinic in Kansas City, I had an abortion. I grieve for a child that almost was. Now that I look back on the situation, I am even more confident I made the right decision. I am grateful I had the courage not to subject a child to a problematic future with a father who was erratic, unstable, and above all a rapist.

Were it not for the unconditional love and support I received from my father, I could have come out of this situation a different person. I could have become bitter and resentful about what happened to me. Instead, I was steadfastly resolute I would build a life for myself I could enjoy and be proud of. I accepted an incomplete in two of my courses, finished them in the summer semester, and graduated from Kansas State University in July with a bachelor's degree in political science/prelaw.

Today I bear a tattoo of a butterfly on my left shoulder as a reminder to never again feel trapped by life's circumstances. I make my own choices.

WKRP in Cincinnati was a popular TV sitcom that ran from 1978 to 1982 about the misadventures of the staff of a struggling AM radio station that changes its format from easy listening music to rock and roll. One of the best loved episodes was a Thanksgiving turkey giveaway promotion. The station hired a helicopter to drop free turkeys over Cincinnati homes. The general manager of the station's parting words were,

"God is my witness,
I thought turkeys could fly."

CHAPTER 19
KJCK in Junction City

When I graduated from K-State, I went to work for an agency that taught young people job hunting and interviewing skills. Ironically, I had to employ the skills myself when the federal funding for the program ended a year later in 1980.

One day I found a listing in the Junction City *Daily Union* newspaper for an operator for religious programming 5:30 a.m. to 12:00 p.m. on Sundays at our local AM radio station, KJCK. It wasn't exactly a position in my career path, but I figured what the hell? It was only on Sundays, and I could continue my job search during the week.

I applied for the position, was hired, and began working within a week. I had to cue up and broadcast prerecorded religious programs on albums and reel-to-reel tapes. At the end of the shift, I would announce the last program and connect to a live feed from services at the First Baptist Church. I was surprised at how quickly I became comfortable operating the equipment. After one or two sessions, it became second nature to me.

I have never been a morning person, but driving to work in the dark, the stillness in the air from the absence of cars on the street, and the ability to perform my job without anyone looking over my shoulder outweighed the inconvenience of a 4:30 a.m. alarm buzzer. I was alone in the station, and the only sounds were the programs going out over the airwaves. The relative quiet I experienced had a calming effect on me.

After several months passed, the station's commercial copywriter left for another job. I was hired to replace her. Whereas today most commercials are written and produced by advertising agencies, back then stations hired copywriters and used their on-air staff to record them.

Writing commercials forced me to be concise. A lot had to be said in a little amount of time. Our sales staff sold commercials that were as short as fifteen seconds. It also helped me develop organizational skills. I faced hard and fast deadlines every single day. No two days began or ended the same, and it kept me on my toes. People often asked me if working at a radio station was anything like the TV show *WKRP in Cincinnati.* I told them the show was accurate with one big exception: between the mayhem and mischief, we got a lot of work done.

Our sales staff would leave each morning to call on clients. Toward the end of the day, they would bring me the advertiser's details: length of commercial spot, dates it would run, and product information. I learned more about steel-belted radial tires and stereo components than I ever wanted to know.

Depending on the salesperson, I could get a lot of information to work with or very little. On one occasion, a salesman named Ted gave me a bar napkin with the number thirty, John Deere, and a few dates written on it. I looked up at him.

"What the hell does this mean?" I asked.

"It's a thirty-second spot for tractors. You can fill in the rest."

"What do you mean fill in the rest? I don't know anything about tractors. Did they give you model names, features . . . any prices?"

He shrugged.

"Just call the guy." That was Ted's favorite tagline: "Just call the guy. Oh, and the spots start tomorrow." I shook my head and began dialing the store's phone number.

Richard, on the other hand, always gave me plenty of information to work with. The only challenge with him was reading his writing. I would take copious notes while he talked me through what was needed. Both Richard and another salesperson, Jeanine, were a copywriter's dream. Jeanine's penmanship was excellent, and her information was thorough. Neither of them gave me last-minute requests without acknowledging it was an inconvenience to me. I accepted them gladly. After all, we were there to make money.

Unfortunately, Jeanine hadn't been with the station as long as the other salespeople, so she didn't have as many accounts. The person with the longest tenure was our sales manager, Walter Frasier. He was a duck-hunting, cowboy-boot-wearing, GMC-Jimmy-truck-driving, tobacco-chewing son of a gun. I never saw actual figures, but I imagined Walter billed more each month than all the other salespeople combined due to his longevity with the station and the fact he was able to cherry-pick the best of new accounts.

I had become close friends with Linda, our billing clerk and admin secretary to the general manager. She was maybe ten years older than me with naturally curly light brown hair that was clipped on each side with rhinestone barrettes. Linda had a witty sense of humor and an infectious laugh. When she laughed, I could hear her in my office, even though we were at opposite ends of the station, and it made me smile.

One day I was in her office when her mood turned uncharacteristically serious.

"Cynthia, I need to warn you about Walter. First, if you go into his office, mind your feet. He has a spittoon on the floor next to his desk, and you do not want to kick that puppy over accidentally." Then she lowered her voice to a whisper and leaned forward. "Also, he tends to make women uncomfortable with all his crude jokes. There have been many women who have refused to even be alone with him."

"Thanks for the warning," I said nodding. I had heard Walter's dumb jokes, and I thought, *I survived the rape. I survived the abortion. I would never allow myself to be intimidated by a man again, especially not working at a job I have grown to love.* "I can handle Mr. Frasier."

"Just be careful."

"Gotcha. Thanks."

Not long after our conversation, Walter was in my office, and I was writing notes for a furniture store spot.

"Length?" I asked.

"Sixty seconds." When he said seconds, brown spittle dropped on the paper I was writing on. I paused for a beat. Not wanting to embarrass him, I calmly grabbed a tissue, blotted the page, and kept writing. I thought, *Okay, it's gross, but no biggie.*

When it happened another day, I knew I had to nip it in the bud. As politely as I could manage, I told him, "I would appreciate you taking the tobacco out of your mouth before you talk to me." He reacted as if he didn't see the problem and just shrugged.

"Well, okay," he said.

Tobacco spittle was the tip of the iceberg. It was nearing five o'clock one evening when Walter brought me information about a new client. He was clearly excited because they bought commercials to run for several months.

"He'll need at least three or four different spots," he said.

"These are thirties, right?"

"Yeah, the wording can be similar, but have different DJs record them." As he talked, he kept shifting his weight from one leg to the other. Then out of the corner of my eye, I realized weight wasn't the only thing he was shifting. He was grabbing the crotch of his pants. I immediately stopped writing.

"What are you doing?"

"Huh?"

"What's going on with your pants?"

"What do you mean?"

"Honey, I don't know what you've got going on down there, but you need to leave now." He looked at me with a blank expression. "You can come back and see me when you've sorted yourself out." He reluctantly picked up his notes and went back to his office. It was after five o'clock now, and Linda had gone home for the day.

The next morning, I waited until all the salespeople left and I saw the general manager heading off to some Kiwanis/Lions Club/Chamber of Commerce type meeting. I rounded the corner to Linda's office and dropped into the chair opposite her desk.

"I had a run-in with Walter yesterday."

"I warned you," she said smiling.

"No, you did not. You said he made some women feel uncomfortable. Calling it 'uncomfortable' is tap dancing around the issue. He was rearranging himself. That's light years beyond 'uncomfortable.' That's like in a galaxy far, far away." Linda started laughing, and I had to laugh too. "Okay, okay. I know I'm laughing, but this shit is not funny." Now she was having trouble catching her breath. I flattened my hand and held it up to the side of my face. "Linda, sitting at my desk, I was at eye level to his crotch."

"Stop, stop. You're killing me," she said, pounding her desk. "So, what did you think I was warning you about?"

"I thought you meant he might try to hit on me or something. I knew I could shut that shit down quick. There is no way on God's green earth I would have ever imagined him juggling his balls in my face. Give a girl a heads-up!"

Between gasps for air, she asked, "What did you do?"

"I told him to go figure out whatever the hell was going on in his pants and come back when it was resolved."

"I can't believe you confronted him."

"I don't care how much that man bills; that kind of behavior is unacceptable on multiple levels. It's well beyond 'uncomfortable.' It's waaaay down the road to heinous. Yes, that's the word: heinous. And he shouldn't be allowed to get away with it."

Now that Walter knew I would call him on his shit, he treated me with a lot more respect. I'm sure he still told his crude little jokes, but he was smart enough not to do it in my presence anymore. I tried to be discreet about what happened. I still had to work with the man. Linda was the only person I told. But all it took was for one FM station DJ to find out about it, and that was the end of discretion. I was getting high-fives from people right and left.

Soon after, our AM station program director, Mark, appeared in the doorway to my office. His cheeks were flushed. He was stroking his blond beard with a smile that went from ear to ear.

"So, what happened with Walter?" he asked.

I held up my index finger. "Oh, no, no, no. Don't even pretend for one minute you haven't gotten the complete rundown from Linda."

He laughed.

"Yeah, but I'd rather hear it from you," he said. So I obliged him.

No friendship is an accident.

~O. HENRY

CHAPTER 20

Winter, Spring, Summer, or Fall; All You've Got to Do Is Call

Early afternoon was the absolute best time in my work day. I had been with the radio station for a few years and settled into a routine. Each day, I tried to write all the commercial spots with more immediate deadlines in the morning—even working several days in advance of the air dates in case I got slammed with new copy requests at the last minute. By noon, all the sales staff were out in the field. The offices were quiet except for the monitors that allowed us to hear what was on air at the time.

During those afternoons, Mark and I had conversations that ran the gamut from serious to silly. I remember two things the most about our discussions. The first was that in the beginning, I would tease Mark mercilessly about the twang of country music being broadcast on our AM station.

"My father loves country music as much as his oldies and rhythm and blues," I said, "but he was only allowed to listen to it when he was in the garage working on cars because none of the rest of us in the family could stand to hear it."

"I'm willing to bet that if you experience some of these contemporary artists, you won't feel the same way," he said. Mark was passionate about country music and challenged me to try the AM station monitor for a while. After listening for a few weeks, I developed an appreciation for the music.

As a writer, I could respect the craft involved in songs that tell stories that evoke incredible emotion. I realized themes of devotion, betrayal, joy, heartache, and desire are not exclusive to any ethnicity, gender, or socioeconomic group. They are universal to all of us as human beings.

Not long after I began working at the station, I was sitting across the desk from Mark in his office. He had just finished a daily program called *Swap* Shop—an on-air garage sale where people called into the station to list items they wanted to buy, sell, or give away. Hosting *Swap Shop* made Mark a local celebrity indicative of the sense of close community in small-town Middle America.

"You know, I've never been around many Black people before," Mark said leaning back in his chair. He was raised in Hillsboro, Kansas, and his wife had been raised in Western Kansas. His first interaction with Black people was with athletes in college. I understood. While I was going to school at K-State—with its nearly 90 percent white student population—many people told me I was the first Black person they had ever met. "I've mostly just seen Black people on television," he continued, "and I get the impression Black men don't treat women well. Is that true?"

I thought about my previous encounters. Sometimes people seemed to expect me to speak for an entire race of people, which is impossible. It would make me angry that they would try to put me in a position like that, but I didn't get the sense that was what Mark was looking for. He wanted my opinion as an individual. I valued our friendship and wanted him to feel comfortable asking me questions. Daddy had taught me to be respectful in situations like this. I sat back in my chair and sipped my coffee while choosing my words carefully.

"No, I think a dog is a dog, no matter what color he is," I finally said. "I've had plenty of white friends who cried the blues to me about their boyfriends. Television is full of negative stereotypes. Black men are always portrayed as criminals. And what's worse, the few Black women who aren't portrayed as prostitutes are either maids or nannies. What about all the Black women doctors, lawyers, scientists, you know—professionals." He raised his eyebrows and nodded his head.

In conversations I had with Mark, we seemed to be able to solve most of the world's problems . . . if people had listened to us.

After four and a half years working at the station, I was now continuity director (great title, lousy pay). Several advertisers liked my voice, and I recorded commercials for them which was fun. I had a little experience with on-air work doing the Sunday morning programs. One day I was discussing my frustration with my friend Annette.

"It's a shame really. I love my job at the station," I told her. "I just don't see much future for me if I stay there. The only possible new opportunity would be in sales. But if I worked for Walter Frasier, you would eventually see me on the six o'clock news. The lead-in would be "woman at local radio station strangles sales manager." She laughed.

"Maybe you should make an appointment to see Mrs. Twiss," Annette said. Annette had been working in the dean's office of the College of Arts and Sciences at K-State for many years. Mrs. Twiss was my prelaw academic advisor when I was in school there. It was an excellent idea.

Mrs. Twiss introduced me to a degree program at the University of Southern California, where I could earn a masters degree in public administration that would qualify me for management in any form of government, along with a masters certificate in judicial administration, an emerging field in the mid-1980s. Judges found they were spending a lot of time on administrative duties like calendaring cases and jury management. Administrators were being trained to lessen the judges' burdens and free their time for adjudicating cases.

I applied to the program and was fortunate enough to be accepted. Now the hard part—saying goodbye to everything familiar to me—was about to begin. I had never lived in a metropolitan area, and I didn't know a single person in Los Angeles. But I had visited my brother Cyril many times when he was stationed in California in the United States Navy, and I knew I would love living there. I had always lived in places with brutal winters. I was fed up with driving on ice and freezing my ass off in the snow.

On the afternoon of my last day at the radio station, the KJCK staff had a celebration for me. I was totally cool all day. But when the day ended, I knew it would be especially hard to say goodbye to Mark, so I strategically planned my exit. I waited until he had an open microphone and was talking on the air. I rushed down the stairs and passed the control room window, waved at him quickly, rounded the corner, and beelined for the back door. I mean, I was really moving. Apparently, I wasn't moving fast enough because before I hit the door, I heard, "Cynthia! Cynthia!"

When I realized it was Mark's voice, I stopped dead in my tracks and began sobbing uncontrollably. Mark told me later he was relieved. Because I had not been emotional during the day, he thought I wasn't going to miss him. It wasn't true. We had become friends, and it was hard for me to leave that behind.

My last two semesters at K-State had been traumatic. The job at KJCK may have been challenging at times, but I was surrounded by good people. I now understand I was there for a reason. I needed to learn how to have fun again. I owe a debt of gratitude to the DJs, sales staff, admin staff, newscasters, program directors, operations manager, and engineer. My years at KJCK allowed me the time and environment I needed to begin to heal.

There is no failure. Only feedback.

~ROBERT ALLEN

CHAPTER 21

Driving Lesson

In preparation for my move from Junction City to Los Angeles in the fall of 1985, I traded in my gas-guzzling chocolate brown 1979 Ford Granada with the Landau roof that I Armor All'ed every Saturday morning for a pumpkin orange 1981 Plymouth Horizon Miser. I had legitimate reasons for giving up my sweet ride for such a butt-ugly tin can. Theoretically, the Horizon would be able to pass California's strict anti-smog regulations, whereas my Granada would not. It would also save money on gas. The problem was the Horizon was a manual transmission. I had only driven automatic transmissions.

My father accompanied me to the car sales lot. We walked up and down row after row of cars. The Horizon was the only compact car that interested me. Daddy saw me staring at the car.

"Don't worry about the transmission. I'll teach you how to drive a stick," he said. My sister Devereaux recently bought a canary yellow Volkswagen Bug with rainbows painted on each side. She mentioned Daddy had given her driving lessons. She was thrilled with her purchase and was now shifting gears like a pro. So I reluctantly said goodbye to my Granada, and Daddy drove the Horizon off the sales lot. The plan was for me to take his truck home until I had enough practice with the manual shift to drive the Horizon.

We waited until the weekend for my first lesson. Daddy picked me up at my apartment and drove to Highway 18, a quiet stretch of two-lane highway near my parents' house. I got into the driver's seat.

"The pattern of the gears is printed right here on the handle," he said. "Before you put the car in first gear, though, you need to engage the clutch. It's a coordination thing. Once the car is in gear, bring your foot up off the clutch slowly to move forward. But you also have to watch the gauge on the dash for your RPMs so you know when it's time to shift again. Ready to try?"

"Sure!" I was excited. I envisioned myself shifting gears like a race car driver in no time. I turned the ignition switch and revved the engine slightly. I stepped on the clutch, moved the gear shift into first, then tried lifting my foot off the clutch. The car jerked back and forth. Then the engine turned off abruptly. This happened several times before I got the car to move.

"Now, you're up to 2,000 RPMs on the tachometer. You should be shifting to second," Daddy said. I stepped on the clutch and moved the gear shift to second. By third gear, I didn't see what the big deal was about this shifting. But the confidence didn't last long. We drove for about a mile, and I could see we were approaching the intersection of Highway 18 and Interstate 70. I knew I had to stop the car without it stalling before I could cross I-70. I had already started pressing my foot on the clutch so I could downshift, but I must not have done it fast enough. Daddy started yelling at me, "Clutch, clutch, you need to clutch!" He never yelled at me like that before. I was so confused, not knowing if he wanted me to step on the clutch or remove my foot from the clutch. I just froze. The car, of course, jerked forward and back, then shut off.

With my confidence shaken from Daddy yelling at me, I restarted the car and shifted into first gear timidly. I crossed the intersection in second gear and was moving into third.

"You can't freeze up at an intersection like that," he said. *I wouldn't have frozen if you weren't yelling at me.* "We need to get you into a real setting with other cars."

No, we don't, I thought, but clearly I was not the one in the driver's seat. According to his instruction, I turned around and headed eastbound on Highway 18. In about two miles, Highway 18 turned into 6th Street, an arterial street that ran through our little town of about 14,000 people. The first stoplight was at the intersection of 6th Street and 14th Street. There were four more stoplights before 6th Street turned back into Highway 18 and continued out of town.

Imagine the same scene at every stoplight where Daddy yelled at me, "Clutch, clutch, you need to clutch!" Then the car, of course, jerked and shut off. Only this time it happened with other cars around. I began having an odd experience. I felt I was looking down from above at an octopus in the passenger seat next to me. All eight arms were pointing in different directions at things I was supposed to pay attention to inside and around the car, and in the booming voice that only an imaginary octopus would have, I heard "Clutch, clutch!"

Who the hell are you? I thought. *And what have you done with my father?*

The strange thing was, by the time I got to the last two stoplights, I was following his commands to the letter and was able to keep the car running. I wondered if this was what the troops he supervised when he was in the Army experienced. Despite being upset by him yelling at me, I was impressed I was finally able to keep the car running.

We made it to the last stoplight, and I pulled into a store parking lot.

"I'm tired," I said. "I think I've had enough for today." Daddy drove me back to my apartment. I plopped down on the couch and stared into space. *What the hell have I done? I'm fucked. I now own a car I can't drive, and I can't go through another lesson like that. How did Devereaux stand it?* So I called her.

"Hey, girl, it's me," I said.

"What's up?"

"I just got back from a driving lesson with *your* father." Anytime our parents did something we didn't like, we referred to them as *your* father or *your* mother. "I don't know how you did it?"

"Did what?"

"How you took driving lessons from him. He yelled at me the whole time."

"Girl, I didn't say I took lessons, as in plural, from him. I went out with him one time, and after he got through yelling at me, I found another way to learn. My friend Sarah drives a stick shift. She taught me how to work the gears at night in the empty student union parking lot at K-State. That's how I learned."

"I don't know what I'm going to do. I still need to practice more, but I can't be in the car with him again like that."

"Don't worry, I'll teach you."

I had seen a completely different side to my father that day. At home he was always calm and only spoke up when he had something important to contribute to a conversation, whereas my mother's mouth was constantly moving. If she was conscious, she was talking. I remembered what Mr. Aurbaugh said about Daddy being the kind of warrant officer who knew how to get the job done. Clearly, barking orders came more naturally to him than I ever imagined. And though I couldn't agree to another session with him yelling at me, he did accomplish his mission. In the end, I was able to shift properly without the car turning off.

We must learn to live together as brothers
or perish together as fools.

~DR. MARTIN LUTHER KING, JR.

CHAPTER 22

A True Tragedy of Halloween

After completing my Master of Public Administration degree at the University of Southern California in Los Angeles, I was hired as a management analyst for a midsize city in Southern California. The job was going well. I enjoyed the work and my coworkers.

In 1992, I had worked for the city for four years. The city organized numerous employee events throughout the year, including a celebration for Halloween where employees could compete for a costume prize.

Between 8:00 a.m. and 9:30 a.m. on the morning of the event, employees would walk throughout the city hall building to show off their costumes. At 9:30 a.m., breakfast would be served on the rooftop patio for staff, and we were encouraged to vote for best individual costume and best group costume. At noon, lunch would be served on the patio outside the employee lounge, and the contest winners would be announced. What scared me more than the axe murderers covered in blood and the Freddy Kreuger wannabes were the ill-conceived costumes some people chose to wear.

This morning, several people filed by my office door, and I smiled politely at them and went back to what I was working on. But two people's costumes stopped me cold. The first was a secretary I had become friends with named Sue. She was wearing an olive-green uniform with jackboots and an honest-to-God real combat helmet with a Nazi swastika on it. Though she didn't actually say, "Heil Hitler," she did click her heels to "sell" the outfit.

I could not believe my eyes. I knew Sue to be a very reasonable person, incredibly kind and considerate. It was so out of character for the person I had gotten to know. Before I could even completely process Sue's costume, I had another visitor.

The woman jumped into the middle of the doorway in a crouched position. She was wearing a black unitard covered with an animal-skin loin cloth. She had on a big black nappy afro wig with a bone sticking out of it. To complete the ensemble, she was carrying a six-foot-long spear. If that weren't enough, she had smeared her face and hands with black shoe polish. My mouth fell open. I stared at her not only because of the shock, but I couldn't figure out who she was at first. But after she moved around a little more, I realized it was one of the city's division managers.

Now I was really shaken and had lost focus on my work. I couldn't imagine how anyone would think those costumes were appropriate. At the time, I was the only Black manager in the city. The few other Black employees were mostly on the custodial staff, so I asked myself, *Did she think it was okay simply because more than 90 percent of the staff were white?*

At the staff lunch, I sat down at a table with Sue after getting my food. I noticed the Nazi helmet she was wearing was gone.

"Where's your helmet?" I asked.

"I took it off. Cynthia, I wasn't thinking. My husband is in law enforcement, and he has this collection of hats from different law enforcement agencies and from the military. I just grabbed one. I really didn't think about how inappropriate it was." Sue truly looked embarrassed.

"Well, it's a good thing you took it off. I'll admit, I was a little concerned." She smiled nervously. Ironically, Sue was secretary to the division manager in the black native outfit. I also thought to myself, *Too bad your boss didn't reconsider her costume.*

The native costume disturbed me so much that I mentioned it to my father on a weekly phone call.

"She was wearing what!?" he asked. I described the native costume to him again.

"Daddy, I just can't help but think that if this city had more Black employees, or even residents, she wouldn't have pulled that shit. Just last year, those white LAPD cops savagely beat Rodney King. What was she thinking? It's flat-out bullshit. I'm sorry." I rarely cussed around my father, but it seemed perfectly appropriate.

"So, what did your boss say? He seems to be a reasonable fella."

"I haven't talked to him about it."

"It's obvious that it's troubling you. Maybe have a conversation with him."

And I did. At my next opportunity, I poked my head in my boss's office.

"Got a minute?"

"Sure, come on in," he said. He was over six-foot tall with blond hair that was starting to show a little gray at his sideburns. Pushing his chair away from the desk, he leaned back and folded one leg over the other.

"I need to ask you about this because it is really buggin' me. Did you see most of the costumes at the Halloween event last week?"

"I think so, why?"

"Did you see anything you thought might be inappropriate?"

He frowned. "What do you mean?"

"Did you see the Nazi helmet?" He frowned slightly. "There was also someone in a black unitard. I think she imagined herself as some kind of African native." He began rubbing his temple the way he often did when he was trying to make a decision. "Do you know who I'm talking about?"

Finally, he said, "Oh, yeah. Yeah."

"You don't see anything odd about that?"

He thought for a moment, then raised both his eyebrows. "You don't think she meant anything racist by it, do you?"

"At the least, I would say it was wildly inappropriate."

"Come on, it's just harmless fun. It's a joke. I'm sure she didn't mean anything by it." I thought, *You don't know that to be true.* "People like to have fun at Halloween." I didn't continue the conversation. It was clear he thought I was overreacting. Up until that point I had tremendous respect for my boss. Now I knew he was the type of person who thought it was okay to make jokes at other people's expense.

The following year at the Halloween event, a Hispanic woman I knew came dressed like Aunt Jemima. Yes, with blackface. The minute I spotted her, I stared her down. The next time I saw her, about twenty minutes later, she had wiped the black shoe polish off her face.

For the next twenty-plus years, I boycotted the city's Halloween events. I either pretended I was too busy and stayed in my office or answered the phones in our department so the secretaries could go to the lunch together. People may have thought it was okay to act stupid, but I did not have to be there to witness it.

After that experience, I knew the answer to the riddle about a redwood tree falling in the forest. The riddle goes, if a redwood tree falls in the forest, and there is no one there to hear it, does it make a noise? The answer is yes, it makes a noise—a big fucking noise. There are certain incontrovertible laws of nature and of human beings.

March 5, 1991

Los Angeles police officials are investigating videotape filmed by a Lake View Terrace man that shows a group of police officers brutally clubbing a man about the head and back with nightsticks, then kicking and beating him some more after he appears to be face down on the ground . . . The heavy-set Black man*, dressed in light pants and a dark T-shirt, then rolls to the ground on his stomach. Several officers continue whacking him across the back of the legs, the kidney area, the neck, and about the head. At one point, the man is surrounded by what appears to be as many as ten officers, most of whom stand and watch their colleagues. At no time does the man appear to offer resistance. Mostly, the man rolls about, as though in pain. He appears to be crying out. He is still for several seconds. Then one officer stomps his head with a foot and kicks the man. Other officers join in.

~ FAYE FIORE AND PHILIPP GOLLNER,
EXCERPT FROM "VIDEO SHOWING BEATING BY
L.A. OFFICERS INVESTIGATED," *Los Angeles Times*

*Black man is later identified as Rodney King.

CHAPTER 23

No Justice, No Peace

In the summer of 1993, I visited my parents' home in Kansas. My mother was upstairs cooking, and I was downstairs in the den with my father. Daddy turned on the television to catch the six o'clock news. Growing up, we kids knew not to speak, not to move, or even breathe too loud while my father focused on his nightly news. This was the one hour every day (one half hour of national news, one half hour of local news) that a protective cone of silence fell over our downstairs den.

"Good evening, I'm Dan Rather and welcome to the *CBS Nightly News* . . ." The sound of the television faded in my mind as I began thumbing through the pages of a magazine. I wasn't paying a great deal of attention to the news until Rather mentioned Rodney King. Apparently King had been arrested for drunk driving after having crashed into a retaining wall in Downtown Los Angeles. It had barely been a year since a jury of ten whites, a Latina American, and an Asian American acquitted four Los Angeles Police Department officers of excessive use of force charges in the brutal beating of Rodney King. I waited until after the news hour was over before commenting.

"Rodney King just cannot seem to get it together," I said.

"Maybe they hit him in the head too many times," Daddy said. I had heard so many tasteless Rodney King jokes over the years, but it was not in my father's character to be crude. I turned to him quickly and saw an expression of genuine concern on his face.

"When I see injustice like the Rodney King case, it makes me think I should have gone on to law school, instead of working for a city," I said.

"Why would you say that?"

"Remember, I always said I was going to be a civil rights attorney. Instead, I haven't exactly set the world on fire."

I was born just after midnight on Friday August 30, 1957, eleven hours after Senator Strom Thurmond (R-South Carolina) ended the longest filibuster in the history of the United States of America. The one-man filibuster in opposition to the 1957 Civil Rights Act lasted twenty-four hours and eighteen minutes—a record that still stands today.

However, Thurmond, an ardent segregationist, was unsuccessful. Congress ultimately approved the legislation, and President Dwight D. Eisenhower signed it into law. These facts, coupled with my fascination with the television courtroom drama *Perry Mason*, led me to decide at the tender age of thirteen that I was destined to become a civil rights attorney.

"You decided you were going to be a lawyer a long time ago because some school counselor told your mama and me that you had the aptitude. You also had aptitude for other careers as well." He leaned forward and with a half-smile said, "What did you do when you thought you had gone as far as you could at the radio station?"

"I went back for my master's," I said, a little puzzled by the question. He held up his index finger.

"More accurately, you got accepted at USC, moved to California without knowing a soul, worked full-time while carrying a full-time load of classes until you finished your master's."

"Yeah, but I still didn't end up working in the courts."

"So what. Your priorities changed. That doesn't take away from what you've accomplished. Besides, the legal system didn't do much good for Rodney King." I had to admit, he had a point there. "Think about it. The Constitution of the United States, which guarantees freedom and rights to all US citizens, didn't stop Southern States from enacting Jim Crow laws. You have a unique opportunity. You work in an environment that is predominantly white. As they observe you, and trust me, they will be watching, they'll see the skills and abilities you bring to the job. But more importantly, they'll see you're not so different from them."

I leaned back in my chair and crossed my arms over my chest. I wasn't aware until that moment how much tension had built up inside me by not talking about this to anyone before.

"Why is it when I meet a white person, they feel compelled to tell me about the first time they met a Black person, or some situation where they behaved badly toward a Black person? It's like they expect me to cross myself and absolve them of their sins. I have a hard enough time being responsible for what comes out of my own mouth. I can't take responsibility for what other people say or do."

"Well, what do you do in a situation like that?"

"I nod my head politely and search for the nearest exit."

He laughed. "You have to realize you were introduced to people of different races and cultures early in life with me being in the Army. There are people who just haven't had those experiences."

"So, I had a situation where I overheard one of the most colossally stupid comments ever uttered. I was the only Black person in this room full of white women."

"What did they say?"

"One woman said she called someone Black, and they got offended. Another woman said, 'Well some of them want to be called African American,' but she thought people of color just keep changing the names to keep white people off base."

"Well, what did you say?"

"I wanted to tell her she was absolutely right. And that on the third Thursday of each month, every Black person in America jumps on a conference call, and we discuss ways we can confuse and confound white people." Daddy was really laughing now. "But it was a social situation, so instead I pretended I didn't hear the comment. Oh, I have an even better story than that." Now, I was on a roll. "There's a lady in our office who told me I don't sound like a Black person. She said, 'The only other Black person I know is a clerk named Jenny at my local grocery. But you don't sound Black like Jenny.' I really did not know how to process this information, so I asked her to explain what she meant, and in a sing-song southern accent, she proceeded to say a few words not pronouncing the r's in nouns and dropping the g's in verbs. By now I was furious."

"What did you tell her?"

"I told her, 'So you're saying that speaking in an inarticulate fashion is synonymous with sounding Black. Here's a news flash for you: I enunciate *all* my words, and I am obviously a Black person.' The woman blinked a few times, realizing her ignorance. It is so frustrating."

"Well, you can be frustrated by it or think of it as an opportunity. I've been challenging misconceptions my whole life. I remember you telling me about conversations you had with that friend of yours at the radio station."

"Which friend?"

"The fella who did *Swap Shop*. You said you helped him understand Black people aren't the stereotyped characters portrayed on television."

"Yeah, that's right."

"It's interactions like that—the one-on-one interactions we have with people—that really change minds. We certainly can't expect the law or government to be the answer."

Blacks accounted for 31 percent of combat infantry troops in Viet Nam and suffered casualty rates disproportionate to their numbers. In the year 1965 alone, 25 percent of casualties were Black, though they made up less than 14 percent of all military service personnel.

~UNITED STATES DEPARTMENT OF DEFENSE

CHAPTER 24

Black Officer, White Army

As a child, I desperately wanted to understand what my father did for a living. After my older brother Cyril took me to see *Ice Station Zebra* with Rock Hudson when I was eleven years old, I became fascinated with movies about the military. I watched classic movies like *The Great Escape* with Steve McQueen, *The Bridge on the River Kwai* with William Holden, and *The Dirty Dozen* with Lee Marvin on the late-night movie channel on television. I was always careful, though, not to watch movies with graphic depictions of violence because I knew the images would invade my dreams and leave me with terrifying nightmares.

When the movie *The Deer Hunter* was released in 1978, I was in college. Several friends saw the movie and told me how deeply it disturbed them. I decided it was not a movie I would ever watch. I may never see *The Hurt Locker, Full Metal Jacket,* or the recent release *Da 5 Bloods* for the same reason.

It was 2001, and I was home visiting my parents in Kansas. I was relaxing in our basement den when the movie *The Green Berets* came on the television. I am not a fan of John Wayne, so I wasn't anxious to see that particular movie. Regardless, I had always thought *The Green Berets* was a

World War II movie. My first revelation was the movie was really about Viet Nam. There was a scene in the movie where Wayne was explaining how a Viet Cong soldier disemboweled someone. I strained to get a mental picture of what "disemboweled" physically would look like, since I had never heard the word before, when a booming voice came over my head from behind the chair where I was sitting.

"You need to turn that crap off! Why are you watching that?" Daddy shouted. Apparently, he had come out of his office in the back and saw what I was watching on his way upstairs. It was out of character for him to yell at me like that, and Daddy was usually oblivious to what was on television. Even if he was sitting in the den, he was usually reading his *U.S. News & World Report* magazine or writing letters. By now my heart had jumped into my throat. I was so shocked I couldn't respond to his question. I just quickly changed the channel.

Shaken from the experience, I went in search of my mother. She was sitting upstairs at the dining room table, shelling peas into a bowl. I knew Daddy was also upstairs, so I spoke in a hushed tone.

"Daddy snapped at me for no reason. I was just watching the movie *The Green Berets*, and he told me to turn it off. I watch war movies all the time, and he's never said anything."

"Well, that movie might hit too close to home for him," she said.

"What do you mean?"

"Just before we left Germany, your father was issued orders to go to Viet Nam." I leaned forward in my chair. "But he was ultimately excused from combat duty because he had a heart attack."

I could immediately see my father's hospital room in Landstuhl, Germany. Colorful construction paper get-well cards from my fourth grade class covered every surface. Daddy lay in bed with a sheet pulled up to his chest. I had never seen him like that before: confined to a bed. He must have seen the fear in my eyes.

"Hey, buddy, why don't you fix me a snack," he said. Daddy was on a restricted diet after he had surgery that removed half of his stomach. Between meals he snacked on buttered Saltine crackers. I spread the butter, made little cracker sandwiches, and placed a stack of them on his tray. He flashed his 75-watt smile at me and I relaxed.

Back in my parents' dining room, I looked up at my mother.

"Daddy never had a heart attack. He was in the hospital for an ulcer."

"Yes, that was in '67. But his problem with ulcers began the year before in '66. He collapsed at work, and after they got him to the hospital, he had a heart attack."

At that moment, I realized just how skilled my parents were at subterfuge. They must have explained my father's absence by saying he was away on a field training exercise or on bivouac, which were routine activities for his job. Whatever ruse they concocted worked. I have no memory of Daddy being in the hospital in 1966.

"But I don't remember him being in the hospital twice."

Mommy lifted her eyebrows and sighed.

"We didn't want you children to worry about him," she said, dropping the last of the shelled peas into the bowl.

"I could understand that at the time, Mommy, but I'm in my forties. Why haven't you said anything before now?" I had recently experienced chest pains while at work. My doctor ran a series of tests and determined I have a heart condition. The condition requires constant monitoring by my cardiologist. Back then it would have been important for me to be able to tell my doctor I have a family history of heart disease.

Mommy shrugged her shoulders in the usual way she did when she didn't feel the need to explain her reason for doing something I disagreed with. Her eyes focused on a glass in front of her. She twisted her lips to the left side and raised her eyebrows again.

"I guess you'll want to know the rest of the story," she said.

"Yes, but let's back up," I said. The revelations were coming at me so quickly. I didn't want to miss anything. "If Daddy had a heart attack, why would the Army try to send him to Viet Nam?"

"It wasn't so much the Army as it was a captain who had it in for your father. The captain was a 'good ole boy' from down south. Your father had an exemplary service record, so he couldn't mess with him on his evaluations, but he was hell-bent on sending him into combat. They would have shipped him to Viet Nam from Germany, and we'd have returned to the states without him."

"But Daddy didn't serve in Viet Nam, so what happened?"

"The officers further up the chain of command accepted the doctor's determination. Once they made their decision, that captain couldn't do anything about it."

After I received my father's personnel and medical service record in 2015, almost fifteen years later, one of the first things I looked for was evidence of what my mother told me that day. There had been times when my mother didn't let the truth get in the way of a good story. Not this time. She did not exaggerate. When my father had the heart attack, he could have left the Army. Instead, he wanted to continue to serve. A memo in his file indicates the United States Army would keep him on active-duty status as long as three conditions were met: First, he would not be required to do strenuous labor; second, he would not be assigned to units requiring consumption of combat rations; and third, he would only be assigned where medical care would be readily available.

When officers further up the chain of command received the Viet Nam order, they reminded the captain of the conditions under which the army agreed to keep my father on active-duty status. The captain's response was, "Assignment instructions to Republic of Viet Nam remain firm. Excellent medical facilities and prepared hot meals are generally available in Viet Nam." His arrogance radiates off the page. Not even a civilian would buy that line of horse shit. But his argument became a moot point. By the end of June 1967, my father was back in the hospital. His ulcer flared up again, and surgeons had to remove 50 percent of his stomach. On July 11, 1967, the medical registrar determined my father was not fit for duty in Republic of Viet Nam.

I have combed the 500-plus pages of documents in my father's personnel file looking for the name of the racist captain. During college, I worked as a clerk typist at ROTC Advanced Camp, Fort Riley, for several summers. I know that correspondence is typically signed by executive officers or XOs on behalf of their superior officers, but I would love to know the name of the captain that hid behind the color of military authority to try to make my father a casualty of the Viet Nam War.

Leadership is the art of getting someone else to do
something you want done because he wants to do it.

~PRESIDENT DWIGHT D. EISENHOWER,
MAJOR GENERAL UNITED STATES ARMY
AND SUPREME COMMANDER ALLIED FORCES
WESTERN EUROPE IN WWII

CHAPTER 25
Operation FRELOC

My father was a strong man physically, emotionally, and spiritually. A tremendous amount of pressure had to have been placed upon him to make him collapse. Looking through documents in his personnel file, I found the source of that pressure in a letter from his battalion commander. The letter referred to Operation FRELOC. Through my research, I learned the acronym FRELOC stands for fast relocation—a mission that began in 1966.

In March 1966, French President Charles de Gaulle informed the United States government that he wanted all military personnel, equipment, and supplies removed from French soil. Over 70,000 United States military service personnel and their families and 800,000 tons of equipment, supplies, and material had to be relocated within one year.

For the United States Army, this meant removal of highly sophisticated and delicate special weapons from French units to Southern Germany. Each piece of equipment had to pass a proficiency inspection prior to being accepted. The letter from the 53rd Transportation Battalion commanding officer in my father's personnel record indicated my father was responsible for the relocation of 1,200 pieces of tractor power and 2,600 trailers of equipment, including missiles and massive antiaircraft guns. The letter goes on to say that as Operation FRELOC workload increased, available manpower decreased by 50 percent. Yet, the maintenance operations my father supervised drew excellent inspection ratings. The letter ended, "He made an outstanding contribution not only with his technical proficiency and know-how but with his exemplary moral fiber."

On June 28, 1967, my father was awarded a United States Army Commendation Medal. The commendation indicated, "Through outstanding devotion to duty, he earned the respect and admiration of all associates. Chief Warrant Officer Doss's outstanding achievements and meritorious service reflect great credit upon himself and the United States Army."

It is a testament to my father's character that he never gave up. Despite the increased workload of Operation FRELOC, despite the reduction in staff, and despite the consequences to his personal health, he not only completed his mission; he excelled. I was reminded once again of what Mr. Aurbaugh said to me about Daddy years ago, "He is from a generation of warrant officers that brought smoke."

No Mission Too Difficult.
No Sacrifice Too Great.
Duty First!

Motto: 1st Infantry Division, Fort Riley, Kansas
The Big Red One

CHAPTER 26

Black Hawk Down

In 2002, the movie *Black Hawk Down* was released. The fact that it was based on a real-life joint military forces mission in Somalia in 1993 intrigued me. In response to a civil war that killed hundreds of thousands of Somali people and created a million refugees, humanitarian organizations delivered tons of food and medical supplies to assist the millions of starving Somali citizens. However, General Mohamed Farrah Aidid, the nation's self-proclaimed leader, and the Somali militia seized the supplies and refused to distribute them to the people. Three elite teams of the United States Army—Delta Force, the 75th Ranger Regiment, and the 160th Special Operations Aviation Regiment (SOARs)—joined forces with United States Navy's Sea, Air, and Land Teams (SEALs) and the United States Air Force Combat Controllers and pararescuemen to capture and extract key members of General Aidid's militia from a building in a marketplace in Mogadishu.

As the movie began, I got a real sense of the camaraderie within each specialized team. They may have been chauvinistic about their unique skill sets, but their training had also stressed that each person had to be willing to risk his life to save the person next to him and vice versa regardless of their affiliation. General William Garrison, portrayed by Sam Shepard, briefed the teams on the mission. Delta Force helicopters would assault the target and secure the militia inside the building. The Rangers would then repel from SOARs Black Hawk helicopters and set up a four-corner defensive perimeter around the target building. Meanwhile a convoy of nine Humvees and three five-ton trucks would arrive at the building to take the assault team and their prisoners back to the base. SOARs would provide air support, conducting strafing runs to neutralize any militia that might attack the convoy during the extraction. The entire mission would take no more than thirty minutes.

Prior to the teams leaving the base at 3:32 p.m. on Sunday, October 3, 1993, General Garrison said, "Remember, no one gets left behind."

The teams encountered heavy gunfire from the Somali militia. When I anticipated the damage that might be done by a spray of machine gun fire or a grenade, I looked away from the screen. I bowed my head and covered my eyes often throughout the movie to avoid at least some of the bloodshed. One man had the lower half of his body blown off before I could avert my eyes. His internal organs flailed as they dragged the remainder of his body to a more protected location. But I could not avoid hearing the screams of pain coming from the wounded.

In combat, soldiers don't have the option to look away. They see the destruction of human lives; they hear the cries for help. Daddy drove in convoys during the Korean War. I wondered if he had experienced this kind of carnage. In the movie, two Black Hawk helicopters were shot down, and the mission focus shifted to rescuing the flight crews and the teams protecting the crash sites.

The movie climaxed when a rescue convoy split in half, and each section reached their assigned crash site by approximately 1:55 a.m. on Monday, October 4. At the second crash site, welding sparks flew in the cockpit as the rescue team tried to extricate the crew.

"It's going to take us a while longer," the team leader advised General Garrison on his radio. My heart beat faster in the ten seconds of silence that followed because I knew what they had to do.

"No one gets left behind," General Garrison reiterated.

The rescue team remained in the hot zone for an additional two and a half hours before being able to remove their comrades from the wreckage. Then they headed for the safe zone at a local stadium. I breathed a sigh of relief to see the final Ranger team entering the stadium. Bloodied and battered, they had been through hell to accomplish their mission. This is what these men chose to do for a living, what Daddy chose to do for a living. I was proud of them and proud to be the daughter of a United States Army soldier.

When I walked out of the theater with my friend, it was dark outside, and the sidewalk of the shopping center was crowded with people. We made our way through the crowd toward the parking lot in silence. I felt relieved the movie had a somewhat positive conclusion; the majority of the servicemen had survived the hot zone. But my chest felt tight. As we continued to walk toward our cars, I looked down, and my hands were shaking. I stopped in the middle of the sidewalk.

"Wait up, Josie. I need to sit down," I told my friend. I sat on a nearby bench and pressed my palms into my thighs to stop my hands from shaking. A strong sense of dread overcame me, and tears flooded my eyes.

"What's wrong?" Josie asked.

"I don't know." Clearly seeing so many soldiers' lives being threatened, the sight of body parts being blown off, and all the blood had upset me. Over the years, I had watched so many action movies, and I was surprised how much this one unsettled me. This movie affected me on a personal level. I had a vague notion about something Daddy told me years ago about driving in convoys, but my mind could not make a direct connection at the moment. My friend Josie had no conception of what it was like to be part of a military family. I couldn't explain my reaction in a way she would understand, so I didn't try. I took several deep breaths, squared my shoulders, and said, "Let's go."

It wasn't until several days later that I was able to fully understand the impact *Black Hawk Down* had on me. I was sitting on the edge of my bed in my bedroom about to get dressed for work. My palms were resting on my knees like they had been that night after the movie, and my brain made the connection.

At the end of *Black Hawk Down* when the credits rolled in the movie theater, the narrative indicated that 160 Americans participated in the mission, and nineteen soldiers were killed. The first soldier's name that was listed had the title of chief warrant officer. Daddy's rank in the United States Army was chief warrant officer. In fact, of the nineteen soldiers who died on that mission, three were chief warrant officers. Tears burned in the back of my eyes. I stood up from the bed and walked to my vanity mirror.

When I saw my reflection, I remembered what Daddy told me once when I was home for a visit from college. He and I were sitting at the dining room table having lunch. I don't recall what prompted him to start talking about his work in the Army, but he let his guard down for a few minutes.

"Our unit traveled long distances in convoys," he said. "There was a miles-long trail of Jeeps, trucks, tanks, and other vehicles. We spent hour after hour on the road." He made a sucking sound and removed a piece of food from between his teeth. "If a vehicle broke down, my crew was responsible for staying behind to fix it. And I'll be damned if by the time we repaired the vehicle and caught up to the rest of the convoy, another piece of equipment had broken down, and we'd have to stay behind again." He put another bite of food in his mouth. When he finished chewing, he said, "The cycle would repeat itself over and over again." He paused for a moment. His eyes focused on the condiment tray on the table, but it was clear he saw the scene he was describing. Finally, he said, "It was one thing to do this in a field training exercise; it was a whole different story when the North Korean Army was advancing behind us."

My mouth dropped open. I was shocked. In the awkward pause that happened next, so many questions entered my mind, but my mind worked faster than my mouth. My mouth was not able to form words fast enough. Then Daddy asked, "Could you pass the salt?" He sprinkled the salt on his food and asked, "So how's school going? Do you like your courses?" And I knew the window of opportunity for questions had passed. I could see from the expression on his face that talking about this experience had upset him. Out of respect, I was not going to push the issue and upset him further.

After seeing the movie *Black Hawk Down*, General Garrison's words echoed in my mind: "No one gets left behind." In the scenario Daddy described, he and his crew were constantly left behind, even when the North Korean troops were advancing behind them. My heart sank as I wondered, *Did Daddy feel abandoned? Did he have any air support? Did SOARs conducting strafing runs protect him from the enemy behind him?*

Seeing the movie *Black Hawk Down* gave me reason to ask my father those very questions. A decade had passed since he told me about the convoys. It was both ironic and sad that when I had been provided a perfect opportunity to bring up the subject with him, he was no longer capable of responding. By that point, my father had been diagnosed with Alzheimer's disease. He would get very frustrated when his memory failed him, and I never wanted to be the trigger for that frustration. My heart felt like it was slowly being squeezed in a vice when I realized there were questions for which I may never have answers.

To care for those who once cared for us
is one of the highest honors.

~TIA WALKER

CHAPTER 27

It's Time for the Talk

I was at work one day when the phone rang. My heart fluttered a little when I saw my sister Devereaux's name on the caller ID. She rarely called me at work unless it was important.

"Hey, girl," she said.

"Hey, yourself," I replied. "What's up?"

"Daddy slipped on the ice while shoveling snow and fractured his pelvis. I'm with him at Irwin Army [Hospital] now."

"What was he doing shov . . ." I stopped myself. "Never mind, I won't even ask." At seventy-seven years old, Daddy insisted on doing all the chores around the house that he did when he was in his thirties. "So, how's he doing?"

"He's going to need surgery," she said. "He doesn't remember he's injured and keeps trying to get out of bed." At that stage of Alzheimer's disease, my father was confused most days.

"Well, I should be able to catch a red-eye out of LAX. I'll be in Wichita by morning and rent a car . . ."

"No, no. Hold off for a while. They're gonna let me stay overnight in the room with him. I've got this covered. The doctor said he'll need to go to a rehabilitation center for several weeks. I'm going to arrange to have him transported by ambulance to a facility near me in Wichita." Wichita was 150 miles south of Junction City, my parents' home. "That's when I'll need your help more, especially running interference with Mommy."

"How's she doing?"

"She's Mommy. What can I tell you?"

"Is she with you?"

"God no. She's at the house. I have my hands full enough just dealing with Daddy." It was a blessing that Devereaux happened to be visiting my parents when Daddy fell. Devereaux accompanied him to the hospital in the ambulance.

Devereaux is the kind of person you want as an advocate. She's cool under pressure, knows the right questions to ask doctors, and has been a hospital patient herself enough times to know how to get things you need done. It didn't surprise me Devereaux had a plan mapped out for our father's care after he was released from the hospital.

"Is there anything you need from me now?"

"Yeah, keep tabs on Mommy at the house. That'll help."

"Sure. You take care."

During Daddy's stay at Irwin Army Hospital, Devereaux gave me regular updates. His surgery went well. His pelvis just needed time to heal. I called Mommy a few times during the week. She talked about the weather, her church meetings, her back pain, her leg pain, her arm pain, and she described her gastrointestinal distress in such vivid detail that I wished I could unhear it. I would interject the occasional, "Yes, ma'am," or "uh-huh." Oddly, she seldom spoke about what was going on with Daddy.

Four weeks after being admitted to the hospital, Daddy was transported to Wichita. Devereaux drove behind the ambulance with Mommy in the car. The following Saturday, I flew into Wichita. When Devereaux picked me up at the airport, she was dressed in a purple velour pantsuit and black and purple sneakers. I expected no less from the woman with a passion for purple. As always, her makeup was expertly applied. But the whites of her eyes had a light brown tinge I only saw when she was physically exhausted. On the way to Recovery Plus, the rehabilitation center, we discussed our strategy with Justin Timberlake's "Rock Your Body" playing in the background.

"Daddy's doing really well physically, but he has no clue what's going on. You can tell him, 'Daddy you can't stand. Your right side is not healed yet,' and ten minutes later, he will have forgotten and will try to walk." We pulled up to a stoplight, and she tapped the steering wheel to the music. "He's not supposed to put any weight on that side at this point unless someone is beside him to provide support."

"In other words, we've got to watch him like a hawk."

"Exactly. There is an alarm on his wheelchair to alert staff if he tries to stand up, but he is oblivious to the noise." The traffic light changed, and she drove on. She was quiet for a little while, then said, "I'm also thinking about later. I don't see how Mommy and Daddy can go back to the house. Daddy's memory will continue to decline. What if he hurts himself worse next time?"

"Honey, you're preaching to the choir. I've been thinking about that too."

"But you know what the biggest problem is," she said.

I let out a puff of air. "Well, yeah. Mommy is not ready to give up her way of life. It'll be a tough sell to get them into assisted living like we talked about a while back, but we have to do it for Daddy's sake."

Devereaux pulled into the parking lot of Recovery Plus and parked.

"I've done some preliminary research. There are a few facilities I like. They are all attractive, clean, and affordable."

Devereaux and I were fortunate in one respect. We weren't concerned about the cost of our parents' care. They had always used money wisely and planned for the future. Daddy had his United States Army pension, along with a disability benefit from the heart attack he suffered, and a pension from teaching high school. Mommy had Social Security, a pension from teaching elementary school, and she bought a long-term care policy to cover nursing home costs if needed. We knew it would be tough to get our parents to agree to this plan, but it was what was necessary to ensure they were both safe and cared for. Daddy would be easy to convince. Mommy was a whole other story.

"Okay, so when do you want to have the talk?" I asked.

"Enjoy the weekend with them. When I come by after work Monday, we can talk to them. I need to do some errands now. You'll probably find them in the dayroom. Call me when you're done visiting. I'll bring you to back to my place."

"Okay, just one question."

"What?"

"What's the plus?"

"Huh?"

"The name of this place is Recovery Plus. What is the plus?" I started laughing.

"Shut the fuck up and get out of my car. I ain't playin' with you."

She had shouldered a lot of responsibility in the previous weeks. I hoped making her laugh might ease her burden a bit.

I signed in as a guest at the front desk, and the receptionist pointed me to the dayroom. The front lobby was arranged like a living room with overstuffed chairs pointed toward a fireplace with river rock façade. It wasn't hard to spot my parents. There was only one other Black person in the room. A dozen six-foot rectangular banquet tables with chairs were scattered throughout the room. If there was a pattern, I couldn't see it. The sun shone through the far wall, which was mostly glass. Two sets of doors opened onto a patio that I imagined would remain unused until spring.

Mommy sat at one of the tables occasionally pulling yarn from a tote bag on the floor next to her as her fingers quickly worked a crochet hook along rows of an afghan. I was always amazed that she could work a design without referring to a pattern. She stopped dying her hair when she retired from teaching. Now short silver curls framed her round face. She wore a burgundy pantsuit with matching SAS shoes. SAS: the most sensible shoes on the planet. Daddy sat in a wheelchair nearby wearing a navy blue and green plaid cotton shirt, khaki Docker slacks and black tennis shoes. His fingers were interlaced and held near his chest. He was staring toward the patio, but I couldn't detect what could have held his interest. Neither of them had seen me yet.

I quickly stepped away from the opening of the door so I could compose myself. I was not prepared for the impact of seeing Daddy – my towering symbol of health and vitality – sitting in a wheelchair. My heart was racing, and tears welled up in my eyes. After pacing in the hall, I took a few deep breaths. I practiced my smile a few times until I felt ready. When I approached, Mommy saw me first.

"Well, you made it," she said. I reached over and hugged her seated in the chair. My mother had a way of hugging you like it she might never let go. I detected the scent of Estée Lauder Private Collection Parfum – her signature fragrance. I allowed the fragrance to calm me, as I inhaled.

"Where'd you come from, fella?" Daddy asked.

"I flew in from California," I said. He started to stand to hug me. "No, you stay right where you are," I said, reaching over to hug him. "You're not supposed to be standing on that leg just yet."

"How'd you know we were here?" Daddy asked.

"Devereaux has been giving me updates . . . Oh, wait a second. Let me rephrase that. She's been giving me regular briefings on your progress." I knew he'd appreciate military jargon. He smiled.

"Oh, she has, has she?"

"Yes sir, she says you're doing great, and you just need a little more time for your right side to heal."

I had my knitting with me, and Mommy and I sat working on our projects while Daddy sat patiently in his chair. It occurred to me Daddy never really developed hobbies. In his time off from the United States Army, he was always doing chores around the house and fixing things. He enjoyed working on cars, and it was his vocation, but not a portable hobby. I remembered he always like reading newspapers and subscribed to *U.S. News & World Report* and *Newsweek*. On subsequent visits, I made sure to bring him a daily newspaper and whatever news magazines I could get my hands on.

When Monday evening came, Devereaux and I sat in the front lobby with Mommy and Daddy.

"Cynthia and I want to talk to you about what happens when Daddy finishes rehab. We're concerned about the two of you going back to the house," Devereaux said. Mommy's eyebrows drew closer together, and she pushed her tongue against the inside of her cheek.

"Look, you've got a two-story house," I said. "Daddy constantly goes up and down those stairs. It will be hard for him to navigate, especially with that contraption in the way." A few years prior, Mommy had a chairlift installed in the stairway. She had no physical or medical need for the lift. She just saw one on television and had to have it. I held my hands up about two feet apart. "Even with the seat up, there's barely this much clearance. I even have trouble navigating around it."

"Well, he can use the lift to go up and down stairs," Mommy said.

"There's no way on God's green earth Daddy will ever use that thing," Devereaux said, quickly dismissing her statement.

"We just want you to be somewhere we know you're both safe. Devereaux has researched some very nice assisted-living places here in

Wichita. Your meals would be prepared for you. They do your laundry and housekeeping, take you on excursions, and have daily activities." I looked directly at Mommy. "And they'll take you on shopping trips." Her expression did not change.

"We're doing fine, and I don't want to hear any more about us leaving our home in Junction City," Mommy said. My father, always wanting to please her, would accept whatever she decided.

"Your mama's right. We'll be fine," Daddy said. "You girls don't need to worry about us." I raised my eyebrows and looked at Devereaux. She slapped her palms on her thighs.

"Okay, if that's what y'all want," she said.

In the two weeks that followed, I spent the days with Mommy and Daddy. Then Mommy and I would return to Devereaux's apartment at night. With each day that passed, we were closer to Daddy being released from Recovery Plus, yet no closer to a safe living situation for the two of them.

Over time, we had gotten to know the other residents and their families well. One afternoon, I was sitting across the table from Mommy and Daddy in the dayroom. Mommy was working on her afghan. Daddy had just finished reading the newspaper. He set the paper down on the table, and before anyone knew it, Daddy stood up and started to step away from the wheelchair. The alarm sounded, and there was a collective gasp that seemed to suck all the oxygen out of the room. Everyone knew he shouldn't try to walk without help. It took me a few seconds to determine the quickest route to him. I considered crawling across the table, but I'd also have to crawl over Mommy. So I went around the table, and by the time I got to him, a man who had been sitting behind him had rushed to his side and was supporting his forearm. I thanked the man, but it was still several minutes before I could relax again. Daddy could not understand what all the fuss was about.

When I sat down again, this time right by his side, something troubling occurred to me. Everyone in the room reacted when Daddy stood up. That is, everyone except Mommy. She was physically the closest to him, yet when the alarm on the wheelchair sounded, she looked up at him, then went back to crocheting.

I stared at her until I felt blood rushing to the top of my head. I was so angry. I wanted to ask her why she didn't make a move to help Daddy, but there was no answer that would have satisfied me. An aide came to take Daddy to his physical therapy session, and I took the opportunity to go out in the hall. It was clear Mommy was either incapable or unwilling to look out for Daddy.

I knew Mommy would be angry with me for talking about assisted living again, but Daddy would not be safe going home with her. Since he was no longer capable of understanding the potential dangers around the house, I felt I needed to speak for him. It wouldn't be the first time she was pissed at me for speaking up. I imagined it wouldn't be the last.

I returned to the dayroom and sat across the table from her.

"Mommy, Daddy will be released from rehab in two days," I said and continued very slowly. "It is unsafe for him to go back to living in that house." She started to put her hand up to cut me off. "No, I need you to hear me clearly." I squinted my eyes and pointed my finger at her across the table. "If the two of you go back and anything, I mean *a-ny-thing* happens to MY FATHER, it will be all your fault." I shook my head with my eyes laser-focused on hers. "And I want you to know that I will NEVER forgive you."

Her head snapped back. She was not accustomed to me speaking that bluntly to her. I was done being a diplomat. Her almond-shaped eyes were wide open. Her lips parted as if she were going to speak, but no words came out. I got up and walked down to the front lobby and dropped into one of the cushy chairs. I leaned forward with my face in my hands, emotionally exhausted.

When I returned to the dayroom, Daddy was finished with physical therapy. He and I talked about a couple of articles in the newspaper. Mommy didn't say a word to me, acting as if I didn't exist.

Devereaux picked us up after she got off work that evening. Mommy went straight into her bedroom. Devereaux was changing clothes in her bedroom, and I sat in the chair beside her bed.

"I think I found a spot for Mommy and Daddy at Avalon. It's a really nice facility," she said.

"What are you talking about? Mommy's not leaving Junction City."

"Yes, she is. She called me this afternoon and asked me to make the arrangements."

"I'll be damned. She didn't say anything to me. Guess she didn't want to give me the satisfaction."

"What do you mean?"

"I had a come-to-Jesus meeting with her earlier." For once, something I said made an impact on her.

Two days later, my parents were able to move into Avalon. Daddy loved the food. Mommy began to make a few friends and joined the needlecraft group. They both took the shuttle to the mall and on other excursions. Within a few months, neither one of them said anything about the house in Junction City. They were enjoying their new life. But most importantly, Devereaux and I knew they would be safe.

The LORD is my shepherd; I shall not want.
He maketh me to lie down in green pastures:
he leadeth me beside the still waters.
He restoreth my soul: he leadeth me in the paths
of righteousness for his name's sake.
Yea, though I walk through the valley
of the shadow of death,
I will fear no evil: for thou art with me;
thy rod and thy staff they comfort me.
Thou preparest a table before me in the presence
of mine enemies: thou anointest my head
with oil; my cup runneth over.
Surely goodness and mercy shall follow me all the days of
my life: and I will dwell in the house of the LORD for ever.

~PSALM 23, KING JAMES VERSION

CHAPTER 28

One Last Hug for Abiatha

For most of my life, my mother remained an enigma, as unique as her name: Abiatha (ä - bī ´- ä – thä). She was a caring, compassionate person who volunteered thousands of hours to community organizations and her church. When a neighbor lost her hair to chemotherapy, my mother bought her scarves and turbans in assorted colors so she would never be embarrassed to go out in public. Mommy was usually the first one to take food to anyone in our community who was sick or shut in. But for all my mother's charismatic qualities, she also had a razor-sharp tongue. I don't think she knew how damaging her words could be.

Looking back, I realize a lifetime of self-doubt is rooted in her failure to acknowledge my accomplishments. But I know my mother loved me. I could tell by the way she always greeted me. She'd pull me close, wrap her arms around me, and rock gently back and forth. There were times she would hug me so tight I thought my joints would pop. I understand she intended her criticism to make me strive to do better. Instead, it eroded my self-esteem. It took years of living away from her critical eye before I could acknowledge my self-worth.

Growing up, trying to please my mother was an impossible task. While she acknowledged I was a straight-A student, she didn't treat it as an achievement. Instead, she focused on areas where I was weak, such as my domestic chores. If I sewed a garment, she always found my mistakes. If I cooked a meal, it was too salty or not salty enough. If I cleaned the house, she showed me where I missed a spot.

My parents created a loving, comfortable home for my brothers, sister, and me. Because of their experience growing up on a farm in the Depression with few amenities, they found it that much more important to provide a better life for their children. Daddy's career in the United States Army gave our family the opportunity to experience other cultures traveling across Europe. By the time I was eleven, I had already traveled to five countries.

While the opportunities we enjoyed from Daddy being in the military were boundless, his Army salary was not. It was my mother, a master at stretching a dollar, who found a way for our family of six to live a middle-class lifestyle. She was resourceful and methodical, delegating chores to each of us. The boys mostly worked outside doing yard work and shoveling snow. Devereaux wasn't given physically demanding chores because it could trigger a sickle cell anemia crisis. She learned how to cook but wasn't responsible for preparing meals the way I was. And we shared cleaning and other household chores.

Being the first-born daughter, I was the one my talented mother hoped would inherit her homemaking skills. The problem was I was an absent-minded, socially awkward child who had difficulty focusing. Maybe I had attention deficit disorder, but there was no such diagnosis back then.

I was in awe of my mother's talents and wanted desperately to be able to express myself creatively like her. Somehow, she seemed to just know things. One Christmas, when I was in high school, I decided to paint a scene on our front window. The theme was children of the world. When it came time to paint the faces, I needed shades of brown. I knew my primary and secondary colors, but I didn't know how to mix brown paint.

My mother was sitting at the dining room table, gossiping with a friend. I politely interrupted, explained my dilemma, and asked her to take me to the store. She turned to me and without hesitation said, "Just mix green with pink." That sounded ridiculous, and I thought she was just feeding me any old answer to get rid of me. But I did as she suggested and was surprised when it worked. My mother had never taken an art class in her life; she was just naturally creative.

Despite what I saw as my limitations, I never ceased trying to be a good chef. There was the time I wanted to impress a friend my brother brought home from college. I was a senior in high school and thought I would prepare a meal of comfort foods I knew he would appreciate. To top off the meal, I decided to make Baked Alaska.

My chicken was fried to a golden-brown crisp; the potatoes were whipped light and fluffy; and the macaroni and cheese had just the right amount of cheddar. I felt good about my meal until I pulled the dessert out of the oven. This was when I learned a cardinal rule of entertaining: *never* try a new recipe. It tasted fine, but my Baked Alaska should have been named Baked Washington because it looked like Mount St. Helens after the eruption. There was no point dwelling on the failure, so I stashed the dish in the refrigerator and focused on finishing the rest of the meal.

Later that evening, I joined my father, who was tucked away in his recliner in the downstairs den chewing on something. My father has maintained a 32-inch waistline his entire adult life despite constantly eating.

"What's that you have there?" I asked.

"Don't know," he said. "Found it in the fridge." On closer inspection, I realized it was my Baked Alaska. "Tastes pretty good," he added.

I bent down and kissed the top of his head.

"What's that for?" he asked.

"For being you."

He smiled and went back to eating.

In the days that followed, my father ate every spoonful of my Baked Alaska disaster. Even in the early days when I was learning to cook, Daddy ate my food and never once complained. At that time in my life, I may have had a mother who was my worst critic, but fortunately I also had a father who was my biggest fan.

My mother was such a pragmatic woman. After she suffered a minor stroke in 2004, she told me she was ready to go be with God. At seventy-seven years old, she had raised four children who were now successful in their careers, traveled to eleven countries, taught elementary school for thirteen years, and was prepared to end her life on Earth.

"I am not afraid to die. I am confident I will see you again in heaven," she told me.

I understood my mother's pragmatism, but it was painful to hear her utter those words. She even described her funeral. She wanted a simple ceremony without many flowers.

"If you want to give me flowers," she said, "do it while I'm living." She showed her consideration of us by making all the funeral arrangements years in advance. By doing so, she allowed us to focus on taking care of each other at an emotionally difficult time.

In 2007, Mommy had only been in nursing home care for about a year when Devereaux notified my oldest brother Cyril and me that she had become unresponsive and was not expected to recover. At the time, Daddy was living in the memory care unit in the same facility. Once Cyril and I arrived, Mommy was never alone. My brother Cyril, sister Devereaux, Daddy, and I kept a vigil at her bedside. My attempts to contact my other brother

Curtis had been unsuccessful. One morning I asked, "May I please have a moment alone with Mommy?" They consented and left the room.

Initially, I just watched her sleep. She had been unresponsive for several days. Her smooth, brown complexion was unblemished, and her face was relaxed into a pleasant expression. I held her hand and stroked her forearm. Finally, I was able to form words to express myself.

"I want you to know how much I appreciate everything you taught me. It may not have always seemed like I was listening, but I heard you." My tears fell onto the bed. "I know you worried I wouldn't be able to fend for myself being such a scatterbrained kid, but the qualities you taught me helped me through some of the toughest times in my life. I promise we'll take good care of Daddy, and I'll make sure Cyril and Devereaux don't kill each other." I knew she would have laughed because the oldest and youngest of our family never got along.

"You don't need to wait for Curtis to come. I sincerely believe you'll see him when you get to the other side." I had no proof Curtis had died at that point, but he had been out of touch with me for several years, and I just felt it. "And I'll do my best to live my life so I will see you again in heaven." I became aware of how quiet the room was and that it was time to let go. "I love you, Mommy, and I'll miss you dearly, but you can be at peace. I know this is what you wanted." I wished my words could have been more eloquent, but God knew what was in my heart.

When the final moment came, we were all at her bedside. The hospice nurse turned to us and said, "She's gone." Devereaux cried out. The Alzheimer's disease delayed Daddy's understanding of what just happened. When he finally realized his wife of fifty-five years was dead, he began to cry. All I could think was I wanted to hold my mother.

"Daddy, can you help me lift her?" He helped me sit Mommy up in bed. I wrapped my arms around her and gave her the tightest hug I could muster. Even though she couldn't return the embrace, I rocked slowly back and forth and whispered, "Don't worry, I'll see you again."

Mommy was at peace with the Lord now. Tears came to my eyes, and I cried a little. But I wasn't sad for her. This was what she wanted. My mother gave me valuable lessons in cooking, crafts, and creativity in general, but watching her face the prospect of the end of her life without fear or hesitation made me realize the most powerful lesson I learned from her was how to die.

November 4, 2008

Barrack Hussein Obama was elected the 44th President of the United States on Tuesday, sweeping away the last racial barrier in American politics with ease as the country chose him as the first black chief executive.

~ ADAM NAGOURNEY,
EXCERPT FROM "OBAMA ELECTED PRESIDENT AS
RACIAL BARRIER FALLS," *The New York Times*

CHAPTER 29

Call Him Chief

After my mother died, Devereaux left Wichita for a job in Houston, Texas, and she moved Daddy with her. She found a nice Alzheimer's disease care facility for him. I would visit him from California as often as my job and finances would allow, usually twice a year. But I called and talked to him faithfully every Friday afternoon.

After arriving at Houston International Airport, I called my sister Devereaux at work to let her know I landed safely, rented a car, and drove to Sunnyvale Senior Living to spend the rest of the afternoon visiting with my father. Sunnyvale was the kind of place I imagined I would like to retire to. They had the memory care unit but also assisted living and skilled nursing services—all under one roof. I entered the lobby and signed the register at the reception desk.

"Good afternoon, Ms. Doss," the receptionist said. It baffled me the receptionists always called me by name. I was only there twice a year. Later it occurred to me that my father was the only Black resident, and Devereaux and I have similar enough features to be mistaken for one another.

"Good afternoon. May I have the code, please?" I asked. The doors to the memory care unit were locked to prevent residents from wandering off.

"347," she replied.

"Thank you." I rounded the corner, entered the code on the keypad, and walked into the dayroom. The memory care unit consisted of the dayroom in front of me, a dining area to the right, and living room just beyond the fireplace. The residents' bedrooms lined the periphery of the unit. Sunnyvale was decorated with an upscale rustic style of furnishings: white-washed wooden boxes, oversized wall clocks (with minute and hour hands that never moved), decorative wall sconces, and brocade pillows in a warm color palette tossed onto overstuffed sofas and chairs. Floral arrangements spilled out of milk pails. They were faux but still attractive.

The staff appeared to have just finished an activity with the residents and were buzzing around cleaning up. My father sat on a chair at the edge of the dayroom. He wore a tweedy brown sports jacket, yellow dress shirt, and brown dress shoes. As one of the higher functioning residents, my father could groom and dress himself daily. But he was color blind, so Devereaux hung the coordinating jacket, shirt, and slacks on the same hanger in his closet the same way Mommy used to. Sometimes his socks may not have matched the color of his clothes, but he was always well groomed. The only thing he needed help with from the staff was shaving. He stopped wearing a mustache years before, but the hair on his chin was always in perpetual growth mode.

"Daddy," I called to get his attention as I approached. He gave me a blank look at first. That I expected this reaction didn't make it any less painful. "Daddy, it's Cynthia. I came to check on you. How ya doing?" I reached for his hand and wrapped both mine around his. His eyes had a cloudy film over the irises, but I could tell in that moment he realized who I was.

"Hey, girl. What you doing here?" By now he was shaking my hands so firmly my arms wobbled. I helped him to his feet and gave him a hug. The five-foot-ten frame that used to tower over me now met me eye to eye.

"I'm great. I just flew in today."

"You come from Junction City?"

"No Daddy, remember, I've been living in California since 1985."

"Oh, yeah, yeah! Well, your mama will be so glad to see you. She's around here somewhere."

A pain shot from my chest to my left arm. My mother died the year before. The day after her funeral, Daddy kept asking us where she was. He insisted on seeing her. We had to remind him she was dead. It was awful watching him relive the grief of her funeral. Devereaux and I decided never to remind him again.

"The staff told me Mommy is taking a nap, so you and I can visit for a while," I told him as we walked to a sofa in front of the fireplace. We sat down holding hands. I patted his stomach. "Looks like they're feeding you well." My father had a healthy appetite but always managed to remain thin.

"Yeah, they do pretty good with the food around here. So, what do you hear from Devereaux?"

"I talked to her today." When I visited, I always checked my father's clothes and toiletry supplies to see if he needed anything. I wanted to relieve Devereaux of the responsibility at least for the one week I was there. "She'll swing by in a day or so to see you."

"Work going okay?"

"Yes, sir. It's fine."

"Well, if you need anything, you make sure to let it be known." This was an offer my father made every time I saw him. Regardless of what my salary was, he wanted to make sure I didn't want for anything.

Out of the corner of my eye, I saw a tall, slender woman enter the dayroom. She greeted several of the residents.

"Hi, Ms. Hightower. Well hello, Mr. Pitts," she said with a broad smile. When she approached where we sat, she placed a hand on my father's shoulder. "Hi there, Curtis. And how are you today?" she asked with a sing-song southern drawl. There was something about the woman I immediately disliked. I imagined by the skin on her face she was in her early seventies, though her hair was dyed jet black—too black for her pale skin tone. It wasn't the bad dye job that bugged me, but I couldn't say what. She walked away, and I dismissed any thoughts of her.

My father and I sat and talked for about an hour. I brought my knitting with me because he tended to doze off.

After he woke up, he asked, "Hey girl. Where'd you come from?"

"I came in from California to visit you for a few days."

"Oh, yeah, right. I asked you that before, didn't I?"

I turned toward him to make sure he was looking directly in my eyes. "Yes, sir. But if you ask me nine times, I'll answer nine times, okay? Don't you worry about that." He patted the back of my hand and flashed his wide smile at me.

"Your mama and I are going to be here a while. Then we're heading home."

"I see." I played along and never contradicted him in his confusion about why he was living there and would never return home.

"Did I ever tell you the story of how you got your name?"

"Yes, Daddy. You did. But tell me again." My parents had always said Mommy named Cyril and Curtis, Jr., my older brothers. And when my younger sister Devereaux was born, we lived in Germany. Our maid Heidi suggested her name to my parents. But when I was born, Daddy named me.

"So, after the boys were born, your mama picked their names," he said. "When you came along, the first girl and all, I insisted I be able to name you. Do you know where your name came from?"

I frowned and slowly said, "No."

"A girlfriend of mine was named Cynthia." My eyes flew wide open, and I sucked in air before realizing how loud it would sound.

"What?" This was a new twist on the often-told story. Daddy raised his eyebrows and put his finger to his lips. He leaned in front of me and looked to the right and then the left.

"But don't tell your mama!"

I started laughing. The innocence of his statement reminded me of a child with an incredible secret—a secret he kept from my mother for fifty-five years. This was a woman who could teach interrogation techniques to the FBI. She didn't need to lay a hand on a suspect. When she set her almond-shaped eyes on you with a fiery gaze, you would confess any past crimes. An awkward silence would follow, and she'd raise her left eyebrow one half inch above her right and purse her lips, which would make you confess any future crimes that you were only thinking of committing. I threw my arms around him.

"Daddy, you are absolutely priceless."

The following day I was sitting in the dayroom talking to my father when the lady with the bad dye job entered.

"Hel-lo, Mr. Robinson. How are you, Ms. Hightower? Looking good, Mr. Pitts," she chirped. She then approached us. "And how are you this fine morning, Curtis?"

It was like a bell rang in my head, and I knew exactly what bugged me about this woman. She had addressed everyone else in the dayroom by title. But she called my father, the only Black resident at Sunnyvale, by his first name. Heat began rising from my chest to under my ears.

"I'm so glad you're here again today," she told me. "Are you his daughter?"

"Yes, my name is Cynthia. I'm in for a visit from California."

"My name is Myrna. My mother used to be a resident, and I volunteer here a few times a week. I've chatted with Curtis numerous times. He's such a pleasant man, and I've always wanted to know more about him. Do you have any siblings?"

"Yes, my sister Devereaux lives here in Texas, and I have an older brother in Minnesota. I had another brother, but he passed away."

"What did your dad do for a living?"

"He was a soldier in the United States Army and retired after twenty-one years of service as a Chief Warrant Officer 3."

"Oh, no wonder Curtis is always well dressed every day. He was a military man."

There was an awkward pause. I continued to look directly at her. I suspected there was an answer she desperately wanted but didn't know how to frame the question. I had seen that look in other white people's eyes before. She wanted to know how a Black man could afford to live in an expensive facility like Sunnyvale. The heat had now risen to the base of my eyeballs.

"After Daddy got out of the Army, he taught auto mechanics at our local high school."

"Oh, so he was a teacher also."

"Yes, for about fourteen years." The heat was now above my eyes and approaching my scalp. "I noticed you refer to my father by his first name. He really prefers to be called Mr. Doss or Chief Doss." The woman's eyes widened.

"Oh, I'm sorry. Well of course . . ."

I smiled at her and didn't speak another word. She got the hint I was done with her. She picked up her purse and left.

My father and I continued our perfectly pleasant visit for a few more hours that day. I only saw Myrna one other time at Sunnyvale, and she greeted my father as I requested. I told her a bald-faced lie. Daddy never stood on ceremony with anyone. Titles weren't important to him. But I was not about to allow this dizzy broad to disrespect my father. He had come a long way since growing up in rural Arkansas under Jim Crow laws. I would not allow anyone to deny him the respect he deserved.

Friendships between women, as any woman will tell you,
are built of a thousand small kindnesses . . .
swapped back and forth and over again.

~FORMER FIRST LADY MICHELLE OBAMA

CHAPTER 30

Magnificent 7 Reunion

I leaned over my work table and dumped silver letters out of a bag. The jumble looked like a demented game of Scrabble. I selected the letter A, then two each of the Ts, Es, and Ns. I strung the letters onto an 18-inch leather cord and attached a clasp to each end. When I held the necklace up, the name "Annette" gleamed back at me. I smiled. I was happy with my design. I just had to make six more: one for Charlotte, Denise, Gwen, Jeanne, Marsha, and me. I planned to present them to my friends at a reunion in November 2011.

Over time, I have had the pleasure of remaining close to six of my school friends. All our fathers either served in, or worked for, the United States Army at Fort Riley, Kansas. All seven of us attended Junction City High School together when bell-bottoms, hot pants, and sizzlers were the fashion rage. We were raised with common values and have a shared experience as military kids.

The seven of us—the Magnificent 7—had kept in touch through annual Christmas cards and occasional phone calls and visits. For our reunion, Denise, a corporate travel agent, booked a condominium in Orlando, Florida. I had seen Annette often during trips home to visit my parents, and I went to college and pledged Delta Sigma Theta Sorority with Gwen and Jeanne, but I hadn't seen Charlotte or Denise in over thirty years. We were to meet at the airport and drive to the condo together. On the plane, I wondered, *What if I don't recognize Charlotte or Denise?*

My stomach was doing flip-flops as I left my airport arrival gate in Orlando. I was so nervous. I would be highly embarrassed if I didn't recognize my long-time friends. When I reached the central terminal, a food court was in front of me. I needn't have worried. Without my glasses, and from at least 100 feet away, I recognized Charlotte and Denise seated at one of the tables. My heart expanded in my chest. I ran to them as quickly as my arthritic knees would carry me and gave each of them a big hug. There would just be the six of us for the weekend; Marsha was unable to join us. Gwen wouldn't arrive until late that night, so we waited for Jeanne and Annette's flights to arrive before making our way to the condo.

Our first night together everyone pitched in, and we made a soul food dinner. Charlotte was lead chef since she's amazing in the kitchen.

"This is not just soul food; it is food for the soul," someone said. Everyone agreed that Food for the Soul would be the theme of our weekend together.

"And to further commemorate this weekend, I have a present for each of you," I said, handing them each the leather necklace I had made with their names spelled out in silver letters. They were thrilled.

Each night, we talked well into the early morning hours. We sat comfortably on the overstuffed sofas decked out in our jam-jams, hair up in curlers. I had circulated a series of questions to everyone prior to our weekend in an effort to reacquaint ourselves. I read an answer, and everyone tried to guess whom the response belonged to.

"My favorite car was a 1968 Lincoln Continental," I said. Several people responded at once.

"That's got to be Gwen," they said in chorus.

"You guys remember Big Bertha, huh?" Gwen asked.

"Yes, with rear passenger doors that opened backwards," I said.

"And the muffler wouldn't stay on," Gwen laughed.

"Okay, who said their favorite thing in the whole wide world is being with friends and in parentheses also said gemstone jewelry?" I asked.

"That's got to be Annette," Charlotte said.

"You're right. My girl loves her jewelry," I said.

"Who said, 'The thing most people don't know about me is I love Evening in Paris parfum not to wear; I keep it on my vanity tray'?"

"Charlotte," Annette said.

"No, not me," Charlotte said. They each looked around the room. Everyone had a puzzled look on their faces, except Jeanne.

Denise picked up on her innocent expression. She yelled, "It's Jeanne!"

"Of course it's Jeanne, you guys. Who else would buy perfume just for the design of the bottle? Our resident artist," I said.

As the evening progressed, we transitioned to deeper subjects like the challenges of relationships with spouses, boyfriends, and offspring, as well as philosophical questions like what happens when we die. Can serial killers go to heaven? But we also were a little frivolous like the debate over whether Wendy Williams is a man or a woman. I looked around the room and thought, *These are empowered women who face real challenges every day. They are an inspiration in my life.* I felt proud to be in their company.

Saturday night we had dinner at Maggiano's restaurant. We feasted on an amazing dinner, but it was the atmosphere that made it special. My friends are so entertaining. I laughed until I could barely catch my breath. I felt like I was seventeen years old again and we were just hangin' out at one of our numerous slumber parties.

After we returned home, I gathered my photos from the weekend, uploaded them to a website, and had the company publish a scrapbook. On the cover, Jeanne, Denise, Charlotte, Annette, Gwen, and I are lined up striking a sassy drill team pose: right hand on hip, right knee bent, and hips at an angle. I mailed a copy to each of them, including Marsha. Since that trip, Denise, Jeanne, and I also took a wonderful thirteen-day cruise to Italy, Greece, and Israel. Our plans for a Magnificent 7 reunion at Niagara Falls in 2017 for our sixtieth birthdays fell through because of personal issues. Cyril broke his back. His recovery went well, but I knew he wouldn't listen to the doctors and take it easy, so I flew to Minnesota to distract him for a while. Others also had issues that forced them to cancel. But I know we will be together again soon. There is no stopping these women.

Being prepared for loss is never the
same as being ready for it.

~R. K. MILHOLLAND

CHAPTER 31

The Christmas I Never Wanted

I continued to visit my father as often as I could, but at a minimum once in the spring and again around the holidays. I was working as an event sales manager for a performing arts center. Our schedule of events made it difficult to get away more often than that. It was 2009 or maybe 2010; I don't recall the exact year because I don't want to. All I remember is I felt robbed.

I entered the lobby of Sunnyvale Senior Living on one of my holiday visits and was greeted by a ten-foot Christmas tree. It was decorated in Americana colors of cream, burgundy, and dark navy. There were vintage-inspired mercury glass ornaments and lots of angels. So often commercial decorators design garish trees with too much silver or gold. The simple elegance of this one made me smile.

I punched in the security code for the Alzheimer's care unit and walked into the dayroom. I found my father sitting at a table. He was wearing a pale-blue dress shirt with open collar, navy blazer, and slacks with black dress shoes. Short of the absence of a neck tie, this is the way Daddy had dressed for work each day as a civilian. I walked over to him.

"Hey, Daddy, how ya doin'?" I asked.

"Well, hello there," he said. He reached his hand out. I wrapped my hands around his and shook it.

"Daddy, it's me, Cynthia." There was something different in the expression on his face. Usually, upon telling him my name, I would see a spark in his eyes when he realized who I was. He'd smile widely, shake my hand more vigorously.

Not today.

"Hi, Cynthia," he said – not "buddy" or "fella." He said Cynthia.

I continued to smile, but my mind was on a session with my therapist a few years prior. I could see her leaning back in her office chair, brown curls tousled around her face, reading glasses perched on the edge of her nose, pen in hand poised over a notepad.

"Cynthia, you have already begun grieving the loss of your father because of the memories the two of you share that he no longer remembers," she said. "There may come a day when he no longer knows you. You need to be prepared for that."

I looked down at Daddy. He had a pleasant smile on his face, but he was always polite to strangers. What was missing was the wide sunshine-bright grin he greeted me with all my life. All I wanted to do was raise my face to the heavens and scream at God, "How could you take this part of Daddy away from me?"

My heart felt like it was shooting a scattergun into my left shoulder. The back of my eyes began to burn as the tears formed. When the moisture pooled in my eyes, I blinked ten or twelve times trying to push it down into my tear ducts. It would have upset Daddy if he thought he made me cry. Even if I were a stranger. I had to pull it together. I hummed quietly for a few seconds to test my voice. There was so much going on in my body that I was afraid my voice would crack when I tried to speak.

Fortunately, I was rescued by one of the staff. "We're all going to decorate gingerbread men," he said. "Would the two of you like to join us?"

I cleared my throat and said, "That would be great." The staff brought out trays with cookies, icing, and various sizes and types of candies for decorating.

"So, which candy should we use for the eyes?" I asked. He picked up two of the brightly colored sugarcoated Dots and handed them to me. Then he popped one in his mouth. I smiled, gratified he hadn't lost his sweet tooth. It took us the better part of an hour to finish decorating because he sampled every candy we used—except the chocolate. I kept the chocolate away from him because I knew he wouldn't remember how badly chocolate upset his stomach.

"There, our cookie looks pretty good," I said. But I was flat out lying. The Red Vine licorice dreadlocks we added gave him an odd vibe.

"That's a cookie?" Daddy asked.

"Yeah, its ginger . . ." Before I could finish, Daddy snapped off one of the legs and ate it. I laughed. Now our creation looked like the gingerbread man in the *Shrek* movie that had to hobble around on a candy cane.

I watched Daddy finish chewing the cookie. It would be hard to continue to visit him now that he no longer recognized me, but I refused to shy away from him because it would be painful. I would just be the polite stranger who came to hang out with him occasionally. This was our new reality. A voice in my head screamed, *How can I accept this?* And I never did accept it. I was angry about losing a connection to the man who protected me from my mother, made me believe I could accomplish anything, and could make me laugh so hard my sides would hurt.

For several years after the Christmas-I-never-wanted, I would sit and visit with Daddy for hours. I would knit while he talked in sentences that became more incoherent over time. He would frequently laugh, and though I didn't understand most of his sentences, whatever he said made him happy. That was all that mattered, so I laughed too.

How lucky I am to have something that
makes saying goodbye so hard.

~ A.A. MILNE, WINNIE-THE-POOH

CHAPTER 32
The Long Goodbye

The call I had been expecting for weeks, ever since we placed my father in hospice care, finally came on Monday, May 4, 2015, at 6:40 a.m. I had been awake only for a few minutes and was starting to get ready for work.

"Hey, girl, it's me." It was my sister Devereaux. Between her sobs, she said, "Daddy has taken a turn for the worse. You need to get here as soon as you can." I told her I'd make arrangements, and she said she'd have a friend pick me up at the airport.

I hung up the phone and sat on the edge of the bed, staring at the palms of my hands. I took a deep cleansing breath in through my mouth and slowly released it through my nose. It's what I do in stressful situations. But each time I exhaled, I noticed the tightness in my chest was still there, and my hands were now visibly shaking.

I realized I was on a journey from which there would be no return. The man who helped me with my homework, played "I got your nose" with me, and taught me how to ride my first bicycle was about to leave this earth. Searching for a way to keep my mind busy, I turned on my computer and looked for a plane ticket to Houston.

When I arrived at Devereaux's house around 7:00 p.m., a soothing aroma from her fragrance diffusers enveloped me as I stepped through the doorway. Devereaux's eyes were bloodshot from crying. She was dressed in a purple oversized T-shirt with Scooby Doo on the front and yoga pants. Most things in her world are purple. She had somehow broken a bone in her right foot weeks before but managed to get around the house okay with the help of a big black boot. We hugged for a long time in the doorway. I am always careful not to hold her too tight. With her various medical conditions, she is in pain most of the time.

To the left of the entryway was the bedroom Devereaux used as an office. Five feet forward and to the right was the hallway that led to her exercise room, and then the spare bedroom where I slept. I stashed my luggage in my room and retrieved some gifts I brought for her. I walked back down the hallway that opens into the living room. The German console radio/record player that our family had enjoyed dancing to since the 1960s was on the south wall, along with a fireplace, above which the mantle held several decorative vases, a portrait of me, and purple Matryoshka nesting dolls I gave her from my trip to Russia.

Devereaux was sitting upright on her bed when I entered her room. Her broken foot rested on a pillow. I smiled when I saw she had dressed up the awkward black boot on her foot by hot-gluing a rhinestone crown on it. I gave Devereaux early birthday presents: a pendant with a carved stone moon face set in sterling silver and adorned with amethyst stones and a stuffed penguin ornament with Kansas State University, our alma mater, embroidered on his chest. I sat down in the Queen Anne wingback recliner by her bed. A few minutes later, she limped over to where I was sitting and handed me a beautiful purple pen.

"It's lovely," I said and placed it on the nightstand. "Thanks."

"No, take the cap off," she said.

I obliged and exposed a sharp stiletto blade. I looked up at her with an expression that said, *What the fuck am I supposed to do with this?*

"It's for protection," she explained. "Keep it in your purse. But when you use it, you have to stick it in and turn, then lift up. Otherwise, you'll just piss the guy off."

Devereaux had this perception that California was a dangerous place. Yes, when I lived in Los Angeles, I was mugged, and yes, my home was broken into. But I had lived in a quiet Orange County suburb for over twenty-five years. I couldn't imagine any scenario where I would need such a thing, but I thanked her again and later buried the "pen" in my suitcase.

Our oldest brother Cyril arrived several hours after I did from Minnesota. I gave him a big hug, and somehow, he seemed even taller than his six-foot frame. He was wearing a black T-shirt and blue jeans. He read somewhere that Steve Jobs only wore black to eliminate one decision for the day. So now Cyril only wears black. He wanted to be briefed on my father's condition; he was a retired United States Navy master chief petty officer, and some habits are hard to break.

We made a bed for him on the living room sofa, and then I returned to my bedroom. In the quiet, I began to anticipate the next day. Knowing Devereaux's bedroom and mine shared a wall, I sat on the edge of the bed and held a pillow to my face so she couldn't hear my wailing cries.

We arrived at the Alzheimer's care facility around 9:00 a.m. the next morning. There was an odd, open space where Daddy's roommate's bed used to be. We soon learned they had moved his roommate to another space to give us privacy. A hospice nurse was sitting at the foot of Daddy's bed on a wooden chair. The room was dark, yet there were two picture windows along the north wall. Devereaux and I had the same thought because we both started pulling open curtains without saying a word. Sunlight flooded in and warmed the atmosphere of the room.

Daddy looked like he was sleeping, but his eyes and mouth were open. Eerie. His frame seemed small. It was evident he had lost some weight. But it was more than that. Lying in bed, he looked so much shorter. Up to that point, Daddy's body had been in good health for an eighty-seven-year-old man. His only problem was the Alzheimer's disease, which had robbed him of his memories and diminished his cognitive skills. The last time I visited three months prior, he barely talked to me at all.

I sat on the bed next to Daddy and reached under the covers to hold his hand in mine. His skin was smooth and warm. I remained there for hours stroking his forearm. Devereaux had attached a speaker to her cell phone so she could play "his" music—the music he enjoyed from the 1950s and '60s. We maintained a vigil with the music of Sam & Dave singing "Hold on, I'm Coming" and "Soul Man" and Dinah Washington's "Baby, You've Got What It Takes" playing in the background.

My back began to hurt after sitting on the bed with Daddy for so long. Cyril had positioned himself in an overstuffed chair in the corner and was working on something on his iPad. I took the only chair left next to the hospice nurse. Big mistake. The nurse was a slender woman with long curly blond hair and wire-rimmed glasses that rested on her sharp nose. She started rambling on to me about her husband, each of her four kids—pretty much her full life story. I was polite to the woman, nodding and acting like I followed her one-sided conversation. This went on for what seemed like an eternity.

Devereaux had taken my place on the bed next to Daddy. She had observed earlier that he was only breathing through his mouth. She knew his throat would become dry, so she requested ice chips that she held above him and allowed the cool water to drip into his mouth as they melted. She also applied balm to his lips to keep them moist.

Occasionally, Devereaux would dart her eyes in my direction. Her left eyebrow was raised, and her eyes looked like they could sear flesh. It was the look Mommy used to give us when we acted badly in public.

"I need to check on something at the front desk," she said. She handed me the cup of ice and left the room. When she returned, she took over holding the ice.

A few minutes later, the head nurse, Rachel, a middle-aged Black woman who always wore a pretty flower in her wig, entered and asked the hospice nurse if she could talk to her in the hall. The nurse exited the room and did not return.

"That woman was getting on my last nerve," Devereaux said. "I told Rachel we don't need to be listening to her bullshit at a time like this." She was right. I hadn't realized how tense my body had been. After the nurse left, my stress level dropped dramatically.

"I know I've told you this many times before," I said while watching Devereaux attend to Daddy, "but I will be forever grateful to you for all you have done for Daddy. It's been reassuring to know he was being taking care of all these years."

"I feel like I'm paying him back," she said. "All those nights when I was sick with sickle cell pain, it was Daddy who sat up with me. One time, I remember I woke up and saw his eyes were closed. I thought he had fallen asleep until I noticed his lips were moving, and I realized he was praying."

On Wednesday, when we arrived at the facility, all of the furniture that had been in the common areas—sofas, side chairs, end tables, lamps—was now stacked up on the sidewalk in front of the building. Devereaux was so shocked at the sight that she drove up over the curb as we turned into the parking lot. Inside, workers were replacing the old furniture with new pieces.

"I'll be damned," Devereaux said. "Daddy's been here for years. Now they decide to redecorate."

At lunch time, the nutritionist brought us ham sandwiches. She had offered us food many times, and we had declined, but this time she insisted we needed to eat something. In fact, the entire staff at the facility had been so kind to us.

I picked up the paper plate and looked at the sandwich. My stomach was growling, but when I started to take a bite, it hit me. Any time I tried to eat a ham sandwich in the future, I would associate the taste with my father dying. I put the paper plate down and started to cry. Devereaux came over and hugged me.

"What's wrong?" Devereaux asked.

"I just can't do this," I said. "I'm not ready."

"Cynthia, Daddy has lived a good life," Devereaux said. "He's tired now, and he wants to go be with Mommy." By now, Cyril had joined in the hug, and it occurred to me that with Mommy and our other brother Curtis, Jr. already dead, this would now be the extent of our family—just the three of us.

Grieving is a journey that teaches us how to love in a new way now that our love is no longer with us. Consciously remembering those who have died is the key that opens the heart, that allows us to love them in new ways.

~THOMAS ATTIG

CHAPTER 33

At Ease, Soldier

Devereaux and I stepped out of Daddy's room to take a break. We marveled over how nice the new furniture looked. Devereaux sat in one of the side chairs. It swiveled and rocked. She grinned up at me and said, "This is pretty cool."

We walked outside the front of the building and stood among the old furniture. It felt good to stretch my legs, and the sun was warm on my face. Devereaux couldn't get over the timing of the décor upgrade. She kept muttering, "I don't fucking believe it," under her breath.

When we reentered the building, two men were pushing one of the new lobby side chairs on a dolly. Devereaux asked them, "Can you follow us, please?" with the sweet tone of voice she had that made people comply without question. They obliged. I laughed at her bold move; I knew what she was up to. When we got to Daddy's room, she had them leave the new chair and take the old, overstuffed chair away.

A nurse's aide entered the room and walked to the far side of the bed. She had a pan of warm water and towels draped over her arm.

"I'm just going to clean him up," she said. Devereaux and I nodded at her. She washed Daddy's face, neck, and hands. Then she dropped the washcloth back in the water and turned to walk away.

"Where are you going?" Devereaux asked.

"I'm finished. I was just leaving."

"You're not done. My father washed his entire body every day of his life. Today is no different." The nurse blinked several times, until she realized my sister was completely serious. She returned to the other side of the bed, and Devereaux and I assisted her with Daddy's bed bath. We thanked her, and she left the room.

Later that evening, we sent Cyril on a dinner run for barbecue. I had been craving barbecue all day, and one of the staff recommended a good restaurant. Daddy's breathing had been labored, and he was frowning, so we requested the nurse give him some of the morphine the doctor prescribed. With the morphine, his breathing evened out, and while he was quiet, Devereaux asked me to walk with her to the bathroom at the front of the facility. As we left, the hospice nurse entered the room to sit with Daddy.

Devereaux was done and stepped out of the bathroom. I finished, and while I was washing my hands, Rachel knocked on the door. "Cynthia," she said. "You need to come now."

I walked out of the bathroom to see two nurses with Rachel standing next to Devereaux.

"Your father is gone," Rachel said.

Devereaux let out a wail, and her knees immediately buckled. If the nurses and I hadn't grabbed her, she would have dropped straight to the floor. We walked her over to a chair in the foyer. She sat there for a few seconds but then asked to see Daddy, so we supported her as we walked back to Daddy's room. The distance to the room seemed so much longer. The walls of the corridor were narrower, the lights dimmer.

Daddy's eyes and mouth were closed now, and his arms lay across his chest. The muscles in his face were completely relaxed. Now he truly looked like he was sleeping.

"I'm so sorry I wasn't here for you, Daddy," Devereaux cried. "I was supposed to be here." She kept rubbing his chest and repeating that she was sorry. I wrapped my arms around her shoulders. I knew my father was gone and that I would soon feel the loss, but there would be time for that sting later. My immediate concern was Devereaux's state of mind. It pained me to see her so distressed.

When our mother died eight years before, we were prepared for it. Mommy told us she was ready to die well before God took her. At the time, I had even asked her to stop talking about her death because I could see it was upsetting Daddy. She continued nonetheless.

"Maybe he wanted it this way," I said. "Remember what Rachel said." The day before Rachel told us she knew Daddy to be a proud man, and he may not want us to see him die. But nothing I said would console Devereaux.

I called Cyril to let him know Daddy was gone and to hurry back to the facility. He arrived within a few minutes with the barbecue. Though the food smelled wonderful, I had no appetite.

Devereaux laid her head on Daddy's chest and sobbed. I was afraid she wouldn't let the local funeral home take him, but by the time they arrived an hour and a half later, she had calmed down. Before he left, I kissed Daddy on the forehead.

I knew my father was dead, but I couldn't feel the pain yet. My chest was tight, and I cried for a while, but the medication I take to keep my clinical depression in check—my "coping cocktail"—prevented me from completely breaking down. I had been saying goodbye to parts of my father for almost a decade as the Alzheimer's disease destroyed his memories and the parts of him to which I could relate.

Arrangements had been made with a local funeral home to transport Daddy's body from Texas to a mortuary in Junction City, Kansas, for his funeral service. Then he would be buried alongside Mommy at the cemetery on Custer Hill at the United States Army base at Fort Riley.

The drive to Kansas took fourteen arduous hours. Devereaux drove our rented Ford Escape SUV straight through, only stopping for gas and bathroom breaks. We encountered torrential rains in Texas and Oklahoma. We learned later that a tornado touched down in Denton, Texas, just after we passed through it. At 7:00 p.m. on Sunday, we arrived in Junction City and checked into our hotel.

On Monday we met with the funeral director, Tim, a tall, broad-shouldered man wearing a well-fitted gray pin-striped suit. His bright blue eyes made contact with each of us as he explained Daddy's funeral had been arranged and paid for in advance. All Tim needed from us was to proofread the program he had written.

"Cynthia, you do it. You're the writer," Devereaux said.

A pain shot across my chest as I read the program—a lifetime summarized in five paragraphs. I began to cry. Tim handed me a box of tissues. I wiped my eyes.

"This is good," I said.

"The United States Army has strict guidelines regarding who can enter Fort Riley since 9/11," Tim explained. "We will have an escort, and they will stop each car to check everyone's identification."

"And you are sure there will be a rifle salute," Devereaux said. She had tasked Cyril with making sure Daddy would be buried with full military honors. "Because you know if they don't, I brought my .45 caliber automatic with two clips. And my sister has the bail money." Devereaux had joked with me about this before, but I was shocked to hear her say it in front of the funeral director. But he just laughed.

"Yes, it is my understanding there will be an honor guard," Tim replied. "Are there any other questions?" We looked at each other and shook our heads. Now we had the not-so-easy task of laying Daddy to rest.

Thank you, dear God, for the peaceful rest of the night and for the glorious morning. May we see everything in this new day as if we had been born anew. Let yesterday's worries and annoyances stay there. Through all the hours of the day, may we walk in the way of love. As we speak with others, may we bring a lift to their spirits. Enable us, dear God, to do our work well, also to think of the things that enrich the spirit. We pray that this meeting be one of accomplishment and that joy will be continually in our hearts as we carry out the business of our church is our prayer, amen.

~CURTIS DOSS, SR.,
JANUARY 2003 INVOCATION FOR
UNITED METHODIST MEN'S MEETING

CHAPTER 34

Day Is Done, Gone The Sun . . .

"Come sit in this chair," Devereaux said to me the next morning. I sat on the chair in front of a desk and mirror. She unpinned the bun I had tied my hair into for an easy, no-fuss style. Instead, she began curling my hair. I was instantly transported back in time. When we were children, most days Mommy braided our hair, but on special occasions, we got to "wear our hair down." Mommy would heat the Marcel irons on the stove and curl our hair. I watched in the mirror as Devereaux added curls all over my head. She lightly dusted my face with powder, then applied shadow, eyeliner, and mascara to my eyes. I had been transformed.

Our outfits were complete; we both opted to wear simple black blazers and slacks. Our makeup was in place, hair perfectly coiffed. Then there was an awkward pause. It was as though we both were trying to suspend reality. But when our eyes connected, we realized we could stall no longer.

Before the service at the funeral home, a few people stopped in on their way to work to offer condolences. One young man said a prayer over Daddy's body and then walked to the section of the chapel where our family was seated.

"Mr. Doss was my auto mechanics teacher in high school," he told us. "I was always getting into trouble back then. I don't know why, but Mr. Doss never gave up on me. He taught me more than auto mechanics. He taught me about life." I started to cry because I knew Daddy had that effect on so many young people. "I wouldn't have the job I have today if it weren't for Mr. Doss."

When my friend Annette arrived, I had her sit beside me in the family section.

Since the current minister at Church of Our Savior United Methodist, where my parents attended, had never met Daddy, I requested Mrs. Bly, a lay minister and long-time family friend, begin the service. I looked around the chapel. There were maybe thirty people there. I expected more. But then when I thought about it, at eighty-seven, Daddy outlived most of his peers. I gave Mrs. Bly the signal, and she began the service by telling a cute story about how Daddy would take her car to the shop and return it to her house repaired. When she asked how much she owed him, he would flash a smile. He never charged her for his labor and only a fraction of the cost of the parts.

Devereaux and I walked to the lectern holding each other up. She held onto my hand as I delivered this speech:

"On behalf of my brother Cyril, sister Devereaux, and myself, I would like to thank you for coming this morning to celebrate the life of our father, Curtis Doss Senior. He was a compassionate man who taught us countless lessons throughout life. He taught us what strength of character means. He taught us to do the right thing, even when it is not the easy path to take. He taught us what unconditional love meant. No matter how much we messed up, he was always there to support us. He was slow to anger, and when he did get mad, he didn't stay that way for long. He was quick to smile and to make you laugh if you were sad. I will never forget that smile! He taught us to treat other people with dignity and respect. Most of these lessons he taught us by example because he lived a Christian life. And if you were to ask him what his most prized possession was, he would immediately say it was his family. He loved us dearly."

Devereaux then told everyone about the qualities she admired most about Daddy. Cyril chose not to speak. The service was over, and I held onto Devereaux as we approached Daddy's body. He looked so sharp in his United States Army dress blues, the cap neatly placed over the hands on his chest.

Devereaux stood there rubbing her Star of David pendant between her thumb and middle finger. For years she had always worn a Star of David. When I questioned her about it, she not-so-subtly changed the subject. The pendant she wore at the time had a different beautiful gemstone at each point of the star and was set in 14K gold. The only time she took it off was when she was required to before going into surgery. She turned her back to me.

"Cynthia, help me with this, please." She held up the clasp to the necklace. As I unfastened the clasp and handed her the necklace, I felt a sharp constriction in my chest. I knew what she was about to do. She laid the pendant on Daddy's chest and let the chain fall on either side of his neck. She placed the palm of her hand on the Star of David and whispered something I didn't hear because I had to turn away.

I held it together up until that moment, but seeing her give Daddy her most prized possession to protect him on his journey broke the dam in me, and I started sobbing. Annette, who had been standing behind me, moved forward to console me. Devereaux stepped away from Daddy's body, and I replaced her at his side. I placed my hand on his chest for a moment.

"Be at peace, Daddy," I said. Then I stepped back and saluted him for the last time. "I stopped saying goodbye to my father many years ago," I told Annette. "It was too painful. Instead of saying goodbye, I would give him a big hug, and with the straightest posture I could muster, I'd salute him. That tickled Daddy to no end. He'd flash a smile at me and return the salute. He may have forgotten how to speak in coherent sentences, but he never forgot he was a soldier." Annette smiled. "I want you to ride with us to the cemetery," I said, taking her hand as we walked to the waiting vehicles.

Devereaux tossed Cyril the keys and slipped into the passenger seat to ride shotgun while Annette and I piled into the backseat of our SUV. I was sure my tears had washed away most of my eye makeup.

"I must look a fright," I said. I pulled out my mirror and tried to touch up my makeup. "How's that?" I asked Annette.

"Girl, you look good. Don't worry." I thought she was lying to me at the time. Years later, she would tell me she was being honest. All I knew was she said what I needed to hear at the time, and I was thankful to have such a friend.

Cyril drove behind the hearse through downtown Junction City, all five blocks of it. It was the city my parents called home for over forty years. Three police patrol units stopped traffic at stoplights at different points along the route to allow the procession to continue uninterrupted. At the entrance to Fort Riley, the hearse stopped behind a black Suburban. Devereaux speculated that it must have been Michael, the cemetery liaison she had been in contact with. The Suburban pulled out in front of the hearse and led the procession up Custer Hill and onto the cemetery grounds. We drove around the monument of General Custer in the cemetery driveway, following the hearse. I remember thinking how convenient it was that my parents' plots were just inside the entrance to the cemetery. We all got out and watched as six men in United States Army uniforms with red berets withdrew my father's American flag-draped coffin from the back of the hearse and carried it to a tented area.

The sun shone brightly and felt warm against my face, and I could hear birds in the trees. Were it not for the purpose for which we were gathered, I would have considered it a spectacular day. At the far end of the lawn, there was a small tent over four rows of chairs. Devereaux's broken foot made it hard for her to navigate the uneven lawn, so I held her left arm while her friend Pat, who had driven up from Wichita, Kansas, held her right. After they put Daddy's coffin in place on a hoist, Devereaux and I took our seats in the front row. Cyril gave his seat to Annette and stood alongside us.

The Church of Our Savior minister said some words, and after she finished, two soldiers folded the American flag and presented it to Devereaux. Devereaux and I began to cry as the honor guard fired the first round in the air behind us. We stood up and turned around so we could see the riflemen. Two more rounds pierced the air, and I could feel the percussion in my chest. We sat back down.

Then came the moment I had been dreading my entire life, the moment I had imagined more than a hundred times just so I would be prepared. The bugler began playing "Taps," and I heard the words in my head: "Day is done, gone the sun . . ."

And while I was intellectually ready for the moment, I was not prepared for my body's response. It started in my ankles with a little shudder and then moved up my legs until my knees were knocking. It took hold of my chest, and by then my whole body was shaking, and a deep wailing cry came out of my mouth. I was bent over Devereaux, trying to console her and at the same time sobbing deeply myself. The minister rushed to our side to offer words of comfort.

She might have been offering the most profound words imaginable, but I couldn't repeat a word she said because my mind was so racked with grief.

My champion was gone. I would no longer have him to flash his 75-watt smile at me or poke me in the side to make me laugh. Nor would he be there to encourage me when work got the better of me. The only thing that brought me some comfort was the realization he was at peace now. He was no longer confused or frustrated with himself for forgetting things. The Alzheimer's disease was no longer in control of his body. More importantly, he was reunited with my mother, his wife of fifty-five years and his soulmate in heaven. They would be having a wonderful time dancing to their signature song, "Cherry Pink and Apple Blossom White."

I looked up at the gun-metal-colored coffin. A large eagle with a shaft of arrows in its left talon and laurel leaves in its right was embossed on it, surrounded by the words United States Army and, below, the words *Chief Warrant Officer 3 Curtis Doss, Sr.* After twenty-one years of distinguished service, including three years in battle on Korean soil, Daddy could now be laid to rest.

I said my final words to him, kissed my fingers and placed them on the coffin. I supported Devereaux's left arm while Cyril held her right. As we turned to leave, the honor guard stood off to the side saluting us. Devereaux and I saluted them back. We walked a few more steps, and Michael, the liaison from the cemetery, asked Devereaux to sign a form. I was holding Devereaux's purse, but before I could even blink, Cyril—knowing Devereaux will only sign documents with a purple pen and wanting to be helpful—reached into her purse and retrieved the first purple pen he saw. Only it wasn't a pen. It was the stiletto blade.

"No, not that one!" I exclaimed. I snatched the faux pen from him and handed him a real one.

When we got to the car, we had a nice laugh about how awkward it would have been if Cyril had exposed the stiletto blade. It gave us a moment's relief from the tension of the day, as did the thought of what my father would have said to Devereaux: "Girl, I just don't know about you."

Real integrity is doing the right thing, knowing that nobody's going to know whether you did it or not.

~OPRAH WINFREY

CHAPTER 35
Code of Conduct

Initially, losing both my parents left me with the odd sense that I had been left alone in the world to fend for myself. Though my parents had been in my life almost sixty years, I now felt like an orphan. The feeling was made stranger because from a young age my parents frequently talked to my siblings and me about what we needed to know to survive in this world if something were to happen to them. At the time I thought it was ridiculous and unnecessary. But I now know it was their indirect way of exposing us to the realities of Daddy being a United States Army soldier.

Almost every day, I encounter things that remind me of lessons they taught me. For example, not long ago I stopped in a Staples store in Cypress, California, to have photocopies made. While I waited, I decided to peruse the pen and pencil aisle of the store. I must confess, I am addicted to buying offices supplies, especially pens. I prepare all my first drafts longhand, so I am constantly on a quest for great writing pens. My current favorite is a Pilot Dr. Grip. After a severe case of wrist tendonitis, I found the smooth gel ink flow, larger barrel, and cushioned grip causes less fatigue. Yet, I always have this nagging feeling there could be an even better pen out there, and I need to find it.

I was engrossed in evaluating different pen styles when out of the corner of my eye I saw a young man in a Staples T-shirt rush into the aisle and stop abruptly. He was in his early twenties with reddish-brown curls springing from his head. His complexion was fair with a slight case of acne. He bent over and began nervously fondling some products on the lower shelf. I continued to examine the pens for a minute or two, but the awkwardness of the Staples employee unsettled me. Then it hit me. This young man had been dispatched by a store manager to watch me as a potential shoplifter. Yet, he obviously had not been trained to be stealth in his observations, which explained his nervousness. My blood pressure rose, and my face became hot.

When I was old enough to start shopping on my own, around ten or eleven, my mother sat me down at the dining room table one night. I sat across the table from her in a T-shirt and shorts. My hair was braided in two pigtails that dangled down my back. The sides of my mother's prematurely silver and black hair were smoothed back and secured in a French twist, as wavy ribbons of curls graced the top her head. It was the late 1960s, and she wore a simple sleeveless shell in a wild paisley print. Her almond-shaped eyes fixed on mine, and her eyebrows were slightly pulled together.

"You'll be going out on your own more often, and you need to be careful how you behave, especially when you go into stores. If you're buying something, always put your purchases in a basket or shopping cart. Don't carry small items like jewelry around in your hands. If there are no baskets available, and you have to hold it in your hands, make sure they are visible at all times because you are being watched."

I leaned forward with my arms folded in front of me on the table. After a long draw on her cigarette, she blew smoke toward the ceiling and continued. "White people may try to use any reason to embarrass you. You don't want to give them any excuse to accuse you of shoplifting." My eyes widened. She paused for a minute and sipped her iced tea. "And always, always get a receipt and bag after you have paid for your purchase. If the clerk tells you that you don't need one," she leaned in and raised her eyebrows for emphasis, "you insist." At that age, being painfully shy, the idea of being accused of trying to leave a store without paying terrified me. I took my mother's advice to heart.

Now, fifty years later, standing in the Staples store, I could hear Mommy's words trail off in my head. I thought, *I am sixty-one fucking years old. I am tired of this shit.*

I abruptly turned toward the young man. He was still bent over fussing with merchandise on the shelf, so I leaned in to be able to make eye contact with him.

"Excuse me. Can I help you FIND something?" I asked. His upper body sprang straight up like opening a jack knife, and he pulled at a few strands of his hair—something I imagined he did often, considering the Bozo-the-Clown appearance of it.

"Oh, well, ah, no. No, thank you." He turned on his heels and disappeared from the aisle as quickly as he arrived.

Since the day of that incident, I have not shopped in another Staples store. Despite my obsession, I don't believe I ever will. All I did that day to arouse suspicion was walk down a merchandise aisle. I am an honorable person who has worked hard all my life. I will not let anyone question my integrity. I am no longer the shy child mortified at the thought of being suspected of shoplifting. I am now the indignant senior citizen who will confront any store clerk who tries to follow me. My mother's words have served me well over the years. But as a Black person, I have to ask the question: When does the constant scrutiny end?

People know about the Klan and the overt racism, but the killing of one's soul little by little, day after day is a lot worse than someone coming in your house and lynching you.

~SAMUEL L. JACKSON

CHAPTER 36

The Problem with Racism

Not long ago, I was riding in my friend Josie's car. Josie and I became friends in graduate school at the University of Southern California some thirty years ago. She helped me get a B in statistics, and I helped her write research papers with more panache than just relaying facts. We have a lot of interests in common, like going to festivals, art exhibits, movies, and shopping, which we love. This particular day, we hadn't been on the road more than ten minutes before she launched into a rant.

"I'm sick of hearing people talk about microaggressions," she said. "It seems to be the buzzword of the day." Even though I had never heard the term until that moment, I felt I could presume the meaning. "People act like practically every action is a microaggression."

My personal philosophy is not to comment on subjects for which I don't have a thorough understanding. Therefore, I said nothing. I know that is rare in our society. Besides, I was less concerned about the subject matter than I was the shrinking distance between the front of Josie's Prius and the back of the car in front of us, convinced that in minutes we would have intimate knowledge of the contents of the other car's trunk. I instinctively pressed my right foot to the car's floorboard—an action that was, of course, futile.

"I don't want to hear any more about microaggression," she said. And with that, the "conversation" died.

At my first opportunity, I looked up the word microaggression and confirmed what I suspected. Microaggressions can take many forms, but I was pretty sure Josie was referring to racial issues. In psychological terms, racial microaggressions are brief, daily verbal, behavioral, or environmental indignities that communicate hostile, derogatory, or negative racial slights and insults toward people of color.

Josie didn't fully understand the importance of identifying microaggressions because she is white and had never been the target of repeated daily insults. As I considered her rant, I remembered back to a similar incident with her many years before. We were on one of our many shopping expeditions, this time to Loehmann's, an off-price department store in Long Beach.

"How was your trip?" she asked me. It was the fall of 2003, and I had just returned from a visit to Kansas.

"It was great," I answered. "I got to spend time with Devereaux in Wichita, and it's always good to hang out with my folks." As we struggled to get through aisle after aisle of clothing racks at Loehmann's, I wished I could raise my hand and clear a path like Moses parting the Red Sea. Loehmann's carried a collection of high-end designer styles that ran the gamut from awesome to atrocious. As an event sales manager for a performing arts center, I often needed formal wear for work. (God forbid I wear the same outfit to more than one special event.) I could always pull together an attractive, affordable look from Loehmann's Back Room. "But I have to admit I've gotten to where I hate flying."

Josie looked up at me over the clothing rack opposite me. At five feet, four inches, her head barely cleared the top of the rack. She had fair skin that time in the sun didn't seem to change. Her black hair was neatly cut into a short bob.

"I don't understand. You love traveling," she said with a puzzled look on her face.

"True. I guess I should rephrase that. I hate the TSA."

"But why?"

"In the last eighteen months since 9/11, I have flown three times. That's three different airlines, three different destinations, and three different times of year. Every single time, I was singled out for additional security screening that the TSA claimed was random." By now, I found myself slamming the blouse hangers together as I looked through the rack. "And the last two times, I specifically observed not one single white person was being subjected to the supposedly random screening, only people of color. While the TSA rifled through my belongings and patted down my body, scores of white people walked past me. I began to think, *What about my safety?* All these people were allowed to board unmolested. What if one of them had a weapon or a bomb?" I felt myself growing angrier by the minute. "Timothy McVeigh, a white man, blew up almost 200 people. The Unabomber, a white man, terrorized this country for decades. I pay my taxes on time and never cheat. I serve on jury duty whenever asked. I don't even drive over the speed limit." I had worked my way almost to the end of the rack and hadn't noticed Josie wasn't looking at clothes anymore. She looked at me, her eyes wide behind blue-framed glasses. Not wanting to ruin a rare day off by getting angrier, I changed the subject. "What do you think of this?" I held up a bright orange polka dot top with a Bozo-the-Clown-like ruffled neckline.

"That is hideous," she responded, and we both laughed.

Several weeks after that, I was sitting at the dinner table with Josie and her husband Dan in their Long Beach home.

"Did you enjoy your visit at home?" Dan asked. Dan has an affable manner about him. I get along better with him than Josie's previous husband, who could be a righteous ass at times. Dan, an engineer, was analytical. Surely he would understand the logic behind my observations about the TSA.

"Seeing my family is always fun. It's just the getting there part that's a pain in the ass." Before I could say more, Josie chimed in.

"Cynthia perceives that the TSA is discriminating against her," she said. I paused for a beat, caught off guard by the interruption, but went on to relay the experiences I shared with Josie at Loehmann's.

"On three trips to three different destinations from three different airports at three different times of year, the odds of me being chosen at random for additional screening have to be astronomical." Dan's brow furrowed as he contemplated the situation. Neither of them commented any further on my pronouncement. In the silence that followed, I could swear I could literally hear crickets outside the patio door. I took a few more bites of food. "This chicken is very good. Do you marinate it before grilling?" I asked, but I didn't really hear the response.

I knew the TSA conversation had upset me, but it wasn't until I was driving home in the dark, heading north on the 605 freeway that I realized why. The 1960s Sam Cooke song "A Change is Gonna Come" was playing on my stereo, and I realized that not much has really changed.

What bothered me wasn't so much that Josie preempted my story. Although, that was admittedly annoying. The real problem was she used the word "perceived" as if the blatantly racist acts by the TSA were only my imagination. In the Loehmann's, I gave Josie, an attorney by profession, cold hard facts about what happened to me. She had been my friend for twenty years at that point, knew me to be a rational person, not prone to overreaction. Yet, she believed it had to be just my perception that there was bias. I was angry and deeply hurt at the same time.

When I reflect on both incidents—the microaggression rant and TSA discussion—I remember a conversation I had with my father. I was talking on the phone with him, and when he asked me about work, I told him about an encounter with a white coworker.

"I thought he was my friend, but he started telling racist jokes about O.J., and he expected me to think it was funny."

"You can have white friends, but don't make the mistake of thinking they truly understand you," Daddy said. "They may say they empathize because they have suffered one slight or another, but until they are bombarded with constant messages that they are 'lesser than,' until they lose jobs time and time again to lesser qualified applicants and have their work undervalued, until they experience being hated not for anything they've done or said but for just existing, they won't have a clue what you're confronted with every day of your life as a Black person. That's the problem with racism."

Daddy was right. I would think a long-time friend would see me for who I truly am: an analytical, logical thinker who doesn't jump to conclusions. I would expect this kind of slight from people who didn't know me well, like the coworkers who *assumed* because I am Black, I believed O.J. Simpson was innocent of killing his ex-wife and her boyfriend.

Over the years, Josie and I have spent less time together. Now we mostly see each other for birthdays and select holidays. Though she previously stated she didn't want to hear any more about microaggression, if there had been an opportunity, I would have brought up the subject. And even though it's not the kind of thing you can segue into naturally, at some point, I will address the issue with Josie because I do still value her friendship.

Travel is fatal to prejudice, bigotry, and narrow-mindedness, and many of our people need it sorely on these counts. Broad, wholesome, charitable views of men and things cannot be acquired by vegetating in one little corner of the earth all one's lifetime.

~MARK TWAIN

CHAPTER 37

April in Holland

In 2020, I was at home recovering from knee replacement surgery. I had a number of projects lined up to work on during my convalescence, but most of them would have to wait until my mobility improved. The one thing I could do while in bed was sort pictures, so I hobbled downstairs and brought up a family photo album and an envelope of loose pictures. I gathered my supplies—glue dots, scissors, stickers, mounting paper—settled into a comfortable position on my bed, and began working on an album from our time in Kaiserslautern, Germany, in the 1960s.

Whenever my father was on leave from the service, my parents loaded us up in our salmon-and-white-colored 1962 Rambler station wagon, and we hit the road. The rear seat folded down and was just the right size for the four of us to be able to sleep comfortably in the back.

Of all our travels in Europe, my absolute favorite trip was in the middle of April 1967 when we traveled to Keukenhof, Holland, on the shore of the North Sea. It was about an eight-hour drive from Kaiserslautern. Occasionally, we would stop for convenience breaks or to eat meals, but otherwise, Daddy would drive straight through to our destination. Because my father drove in truck and tank convoys in the United States Army for a living, he was accustomed to long hours at the wheel.

I was nine years old at the time, and I tried to stay awake to keep him company on the long drive. I poked my head over the front seat. The pleasant aroma of Old Spice aftershave greeted my nostrils. I talked to him while Mommy leaned against a pillow on the passenger window, snoring.

"Daddy, how do you drive for hours at a time?" I asked.

"I just focus on the road," he said. I tried looking at the white lines in the road, and frankly, after about five minutes, it hypnotized me. "This helps keep me going also," he said and reached under his seat and pulled out a bag of Kraft caramels. Daddy kept a bag of Kraft caramels under the driver's seat of every car he owned. It was an unspoken rule in our family that no one touched Daddy's Kraft caramels.

Occasionally, we would stop along the roadside to eat. A green and white Coleman ice chest accompanied us in the back. It was filled with golden fried chicken that would put Colonel Sanders to shame, cheeses, bread, and some of the best roast chicken and ham sandwiches I have ever eaten. I would unwrap the wax paper to reveal the toasted bread of a perfect sandwich. The chicken was just the right balance of white and dark meat, always moist and tender, and the ham had been baked with my mother's signature sweet-and-sour glaze. She used Kraft Sandwich Spread on the bread,

Mommy, Devereux, Me, Curtis, Jr., and Cyril

a mixture of mayonnaise, sweet pickle relish, and spices. I don't know how she managed, but the bread was never soggy.

Before arriving in Keukenhof, we traveled through Paris, France, and Brussels, Belgium. I have no memory of either country. But I do recall us stopping long enough for my mother to purchase wine goblets for her collection, souvenir pins for my brothers' felt fedoras, and sterling silver charms for bracelets she had given my sister Devereux and me.

My parents made a reservation for us in a bed-and-breakfast in Keukenhof. The B and B was decorated like a fairytale cottage with gingerbread trim on the façade and, of course, tulips and daffodils in the front yard. The interior was cozy and inviting. We all shared one big room.

Curtis, Jr., Devereux, Me, and Cyril

The only thing problematic was they had no indoor plumbing, only an outhouse in back. It was late at night, and when I told Mommy I needed to pee, she plopped a half-gallon-sized coffee can down on the floor in front of me. I looked up at her.

"What's that for?" I asked.

"That's our chamber pot. You can go in the can, and we'll dump it in the morning," she said. I looked at her like she had lost her mind. Then I remembered my parents were raised on farms in the 1930s. They would be used to using chamber pots.

Our first excursion the next day was to the fields where tulips were grown. Holland is known worldwide for its tulip production. Keukenhof had the most famous and largest flower park in the world—an impressive sight. Acres of land were covered in brightly colored tulips slightly swaying in the breeze, the landscape occasionally dotted by windmills. Each area was devoted to a different color. There were shades of yellow and orange and red and purple and pink—even white. There were hybrids; pink tulips with white edges; orange tulips with yellow edges. The tulips continued farther than my eyes could see. The fragrance of all those flowers was not overpowering either. It was a clean, delicate scent that made you want to breathe deeply. It was at that point that the tulip became my favorite flower.

Our next outing was to the North Sea. On our Atlantic Ocean crossing, I tried my best not to look down at the water. I couldn't swim and was nervous about being in the ocean. But standing on the shore of the North Sea as the waves ebbed and flowed, I could appreciate the beauty. I took a deep breath of the sea air. The crisp, clean scent calmed me. We spent a few hours on the shore collecting seashells and watching the water. Then we went into one of the shops where Mommy bought our souvenir charms and pins. Our charms were a pair of Dutch cloisonné shoes with the traditional blue and white delft pattern on them.

The following day, we ventured to the cheese market. In school, our teacher was reading the book *Heidi* to us in class. The story of a young girl growing up in the Swiss Alps with her grandfather, a goat herder, described many scenes where the two of them would have a meal of simply fresh-baked bread and cheese. The author, Johanna Spryri, rendered the scenes so well that my mouth would water upon hearing them read. I gained such an appreciation for cheese after experiencing that book.

At the market, wheels of cheese sealed in yellow wax were stacked and displayed in rows along the sidewalks. My eyes popped open at the sight of them. I thought I would lose my mind; there was so much cheese. In one of the shops, Mommy selected some Gouda and Edam for our pantry. I favored the Gouda for its buttery flavor, but the Edam was good as well. Dutch dairy exportation was just starting to gain momentum in the 1960s. Today, the Dutch produce and export hundreds of millions of tons of cheese every year.

Finally, we visited the smallest city in the Netherlands: Madurodam. It features exact replicas of special buildings and famous landmarks from around the country on a scale of 1:25. Buildings, markets, canals, windmills, Schiphol Airport, the Port of Rotterdam, Dam Square, and the Delta Works were all perfectly replicated to the smallest detail. Instead of being a static miniature city, Madurodam had moving parts. The windmills turned; airplanes landed at the airport; trains ran through the park; and ships sailed on the river.

In 2020, as I sat flipping through a photo album in my California apartment reveling in the happy memories of that Holland vacation, my brain made a connection that made my body shudder. In reviewing my father's service record months before, I learned that on May 24, 1967, just weeks after our Holland vacation, orders for Daddy's next duty assignment were issued.

In the military, the term scuttlebutt refers to an informal line of communication. Scuttlebutt is more than a rumor mill in that it has a high degree of accuracy. Therefore, there is an extremely high probability that during our Holland vacation, Daddy already knew what his next assignment would be. My chest constricted, and I found it hard to breathe when I realized Daddy most likely knew his next assignment could be the Republic of Viet

Chief Warrant Officer Curtis Doss, Sr., United States Army

Nam. Yet, he never gave any indication to us. He was his usual affable self on vacation. He shuttled us around to all the sights and flashed his classic 75-watt smile, shielding us from his thoughts and feelings.

I now view the pictures of our Holland vacation, our best vacation ever, with great reverence for my father.

Memory is the diary we all carry about with us.

~OSCAR WILDE

CHAPTER 38

Last Dance

When I was still visiting my father in Sunnyvale Senior Living, I grew increasingly frustrated with my inability to reach that part of him where our shared memories lived. I consulted a friend of mine who manages a senior center. She told me to try playing music from his past. So, on my next visit, I brought a compact disc I recorded with some of "his" music by artists he enjoyed over the years. The CD included Chuck Berry, Little Richard, The Beatles, and Ray Charles.

I had just settled down in the dayroom with Daddy at Sunnyvale. He was wearing a long-sleeve burgundy shirt in a plaid pattern, khaki slacks, and black tennis shoes. I asked one of the staff to load the CD I had prepared into their mini boombox. The first song on the CD was "Green Onions" by Booker T. & the M.G.'s. It was a jazzy song, and Daddy sat straight up in his chair as soon as he heard it playing.

"Boy, that's one from back in the day!" he said.

My heart rose in my chest. Tears came to my eyes. He remembered. My family used to twist to "Green Onions" and other favorite tunes for hours in the living room of our Kaiserslautern, Germany, home in the 1960s. Daddy started tapping his foot and slapping his knee.

"You want to dance, Daddy?"

He didn't even answer. He jumped up and started swiveling his hips. I handed my video camera to one of the staff, showed him how to begin recording, and joined Daddy in the middle of the room dancing. I didn't bother to wipe away the tears that were streaming down my face. I was happy.

The next song was "Baby, You've Got What It Takes" by Brook Benton and Dinah Washington. It was one of my parents' favorite songs. Daddy grabbed my hand, and we began to two-step, the way he used to dance with my mother. I loved two-stepping with Daddy. It was easy to follow his lead. He spun me around, but coming out of the twirl, I was out of step with him. There was supposed to be a half-step pause after the twirl. I never mastered that part of the two-step, so as usual, I stumbled. Daddy slowed down when he saw me stumble and exaggerated his movements, so it would be easier for me to get back in step with him. He was always the teacher.

On the Chuck Berry song that followed, we were twisting again. Daddy executed his signature move. He lifted his right leg at an angle and continued to twist at the waist, working his arms back and forth. My eighty-five-year-old father still had serious skills.

"Get it, Daddy!" I shouted. "That's it. Work it out now."

Several of the staff on duty had gathered around us and were saying, "Go, Mr. Doss, go!" Daddy and I danced for more than half an hour. When the CD ended, the staff were clapping. I was exhausted, but Daddy looked like he could continue dancing forever.

I walked him over to the fireplace, and we sat down on the couch facing it. One of the staff walked by.

"Did you have fun, Mr. Doss?" she asked.

"Yeah, I did," he said.

"That's great," she said turning to me. "Your father is such a dear man."

"He sure is," I replied.

"We love having him here."

Daddy and I sat quietly after she left. I was holding his left hand in mine. The music had struck a definite chord with him. As I stroked the back of his hand, I wondered what other memories were locked deep inside of him.

I thought back to a time when I was seven or eight years old. It was five o'clock in the morning. I tumbled out of bed and made my way down the hallway of our apartment in Kaiserslautern, Germany. I rubbed my eyes as they adjusted to the bright light of the kitchen. Daddy stood at the stove wearing a white T-shirt and his olive drab uniform pants tucked into half-calf combat boots.

"Have a seat, buddy," he said. "It will be ready in a few minutes."

This was our routine. He was preparing breakfast before he had to report for duty. While the rest of the family was still asleep, he was fixing our usual breakfast of eggs over-easy, bacon, and toast.

We sat down at the table and started eating. He cut into his eggs, and the yolk ran across the plate. He then used his toast to soak up the yolk and bit into it. I cut into my eggs, and the yolk ran across the plate. I used my toast to soak up the yolk and bit into it. I watched him take a sip of his coffee.

"Aah, now that's good stuff," he said.

I drank my milk. "Aah, now that's good stuff," I said.

He laughed. "So, how's school?"

"It's fine. I really like my teacher. Math is hard, though." I did well in all my subjects except math.

"Well, you'll get it eventually. You're a smart girl."

We finished eating, and Daddy cleared the table. He washed and dried the dishes and placed them back in the cupboard. As I watched him work, I thought about how lucky I was. He cared enough about me to fix me breakfast and ask what was going on in my life.

Before he left for work, I gave him a big hug.

"I love you, Daddy," I said.

I went back to bed and got up again and had breakfast with my mother and siblings as if I hadn't already eaten. I never told anyone about our secret breakfasts. It was a special time reserved for the two of us, and I didn't want anything to jinx it. If my mother knew, I'm sure she would have objected. I sense my father felt the same way. That's why he always washed and put the dishes away.

Sitting in front of the fireplace with Daddy at Sunnyvale decades later, holding his hand, I looked up at my father's face, with the perpetual five o'clock shadow, creases on either side of his chin, and wide, inquisitive eyes. I asked God, *Please let him remember how many times I told him, "I love you, Daddy."*

It demands great spiritual resilience not to hate the hater whose foot is on your neck, and an even greater miracle of perception and charity not to teach your child to hate.

~JAMES BALDWIN

EPILOGUE

When I began this journey, I wanted to learn more about my father's experiences in the military and acknowledge the profound impact he had on shaping my character. With his kind, generous nature, I had questioned how my father reconciled being a United States Army soldier with his Christian beliefs. I never bothered to ask him that question because I think I already knew part of the answer. My father would do everything within his power to protect the people in his life about whom he cared. And my father cared about everyone.

The specific knowledge I gained from my father's service record helps me understand why my father never talked to me about what he went through during the last two years he served in the United States Army under a racist commander. It was an incredibly personal story, and he was a deeply private man. It would have been too difficult for him to talk to me about what happened.

Instead, what my father did do was equip me with the tools necessary for me to thrive in a culturally diverse world: an open heart, a forgiving spirit, and a thirst for knowledge. When I faced racism at work, I was able to put it into perspective. I did not allow it to make me bitter. I also believe my father's ability to forgive made him a happier man in life. Letting go of the past and forgiving makes it easier to move forward, grow, and evolve. I will admit, for me the forgiving spirit part is still a work in progress. I am, after all, my mother's daughter as well.

I also admit that the eleven-year-old rebel who wrote "Black Power" on her blue jeans still lives inside me. I do not condone violence of any kind against people or property. But the reality is, there are white people who will not accept the rights guaranteed under the United States Constitution apply to all races unless they are forced to. Nonviolent direct action is still necessary in this country.

Recently, my friend and former coworker Mark from KJCK Radio said something that resonated with me. In an email he wrote, "My boys grew up in JC [Junction City] where people of a different race were not unusual; it was the norm. And isn't that the way it should be? When will we learn as a nation?" He attached pictures of his grandchildren with their friends— friends of different races and ethnicities. I agree with Mark. Divisiveness will not move this country forward. And I am encouraged that future generations may do a better job of bridging gaps than we have.

The lessons my father taught me have served me well in life, and I hope others are inspired by his legacy.

The memory of my father I keep closest to my heart is the day I danced with him for the last time. The pure joy I saw on his face as he executed his signature moves will always lift me up. He was my champion. And I now realize, to Daddy I was never a simple caterpillar. He had always seen me as a butterfly waiting to spread its wings and fly.